Is There (Anti-)Neoliberal Architecture?

T0327169

jovis

Is There (Anti-)Neoliberal Architecture?

Ana Jeinić | Anselm Wagner [eds.]

architektur + analyse 3

Introduction   6
Ana Jeinić and Anselm Wagner

I. HISTORICAL ORIGINS AND PERSPECTIVES

From Liquid Space to Solid Bodies   14
Architecture between Neoliberalism and Control Society
Ole W. Fischer

Framing the Possible   32
Cybernetic Neoliberalism and the Architecture of Immaterial Labor
Andreas Rumpfhuber

In the Search of Efficacy   46
Debate and Experimentation after May ´68
Tahl Kaminer

2. THE END (AND RETURN?) OF UTOPIA AND CRITIQUE

Neoliberalism and the Crisis of the Project... in Architecture and Beyond 64
Ana Jeinić

Neoliberalism and the Possibility of Critique   78
Rixt Hoekstra

3. CASE STUDIES

Education, Consumption, Reproduction   88
Three Cautionary Tales
Maria S. Giudici

Architectural Asymmetries   104
Gideon Boie (BAVO)

Neoliberal Liaisons   118
Interactions between Architecture and Fashion in the Age of Creative Industries
Ana Llorente

CONTENTS

White as the Color of Neoliberalism   134
Olaf Pfeifer

Baukulturindustrie—A Polemic   148
Oliver Ziegenhardt

Contributor Biographies   158
Imprint   160

Ana Jeinić and Anselm Wagner

INTRODUCTION

Neoliberal ideology has irreversibly changed our world. Hardly anybody acquainted with the term *neoliberalism* would try to deny this. But what do we mean *exactly* when we talk about neoliberalism? Or, who are the neoliberals?

Neoliberalism seems to exist like a phantom: everybody fears it, hates it, and talks about it, but nobody is brave enough to identify him- or herself with it. Neoliberalism is considered responsible for nearly everything that is going wrong in economics, politics, and social life—and the actual economic crisis, caused by a ruthless "casino capitalism,"[1] seems to confirm this objection. But it is nearly impossible to find political parties or even just individual people who declare themselves to be neoliberal. Of course, one will find many of them in the United States, though there they won't claim to be *neoliberals* but simply *capitalists* or *conservatives*, since in the States the term *liberal* is commonly used for social democrats. In Europe, the term *neoliberalism* is, with very few exceptions, only used in a pejorative way. It is a word to characterize the Other and almost never the self. This raises the question as to whether the discourse of neoliberalism serves as a kind of conspiracy theory for leftist intellectuals, comparable to the role of freemasonry for the petit bourgeois of the far right.

But nothing is more erroneous than that. We know where the ideology of neoliberalism comes from; we know its representatives and executors, beginning with some Austrian and American economists

[1]   Susan Strange, *Casino Capitalism* (Oxford: Blackwell Publishers, 1986).

like Ludwig von Mises, Friedrich August von Hayek, Gary S. Becker, Theodore W. Schultz, and Milton Friedman, and some politicians like Margaret Thatcher and Ronald Reagan. But how are we then to explain the unease that befalls us today when we try to confine the meaning of the term neoliberalism and use it in a more precise way than it has been used in the common empty laments?

The difficulty seems to lie in the fact that neoliberalism has meanwhile become the indisputable discourse of our era—something spread all around us and consequently difficult to localize and define. Since the nineteen-nineties, all mainstream media, all political parties, including the Social Democrats and the Green Party, have been doing the neoliberal job. Like a big sponge, neoliberalism has absorbed all leftist emancipatory tendencies toward freedom, autonomy, and self-determination, and all critique of governmental suppression and paternalism formulated in the sixties, fusing them with neoconservative ideas of a *free* (but in fact highly protected) market, low taxes (for companies), and no boundaries (for the free flux of goods, capital, and manpower). In the end, it has diffused into all Western and also into most of the Eastern societies, parties, minds, and economic and political systems. We live in it like a fish does in water. And despite its bad image, we must confess: all of us are neoliberals.

While acknowledging the difficulties of providing an exact definition, what we can do is at least try to sketch some anchor points for approaching neoliberalism. Marxist critics like David Harvey have defined it as a technique of the "restoration of class power" to increase the uneven distribution of capital and power.[2] Beyond that, neoliberalism should be understood as an all-encompassing *Weltanschauung*. As Michel Foucault[3] and others[4] have pointed out, the very essence of neoliberalism (and also its difference to classical liberalism) can be found in its total pretension. Up to the nineteen-fifties, neoliberal thought was limited to the field of economics. But in the sixties, neoliberal economists started to expand their interests and to apply the laws of the free market to all fields of science and to social life. The market became the measure of all things, a natural fact not to be challenged, comparable to the eternal laws of Darwin's evolution theory. According to neoliberal theory, all kinds of social interaction can be explained by economic reason. The most extreme view in this respect was advanced by the Chicagoan economists Gary S. Becker and Theodore W. Schultz with their theory of *human capital*, which also regards

[2]   David Harvey, *Spaces of Global Capitalism* (London and New York: Verso, 2006), pp. 7–68.
[3]   See Michel Foucault, *The Birth of Biopolitics: Lectures at the Collège de France, 1978–1979*, ed. Michel Senellart, trans. Graham Burchell (Basingstoke et al.: Palgrave Macmillan, 2010), pp. 216–19.
[4]   Herbert Schui and Stephanie Blankenburg, *Neoliberalismus: Theorie, Gegner*, Praxis (Hamburg: VSA-Verlag, 2002), p. 79.

the love and care of a mother for her child as an *investment*, because the more love you have gained as a baby, the better are your chances of being economically successful in your adult life; so love is a good investment with high yield return.[5] Today, the notion of *human capital* is omnipresent; it is just one of the countless indications of the present-day economization of the social, whose signs and structures can be found in mass media and colloquial language. Thinking and arguing in this way does not sound inhuman but *realistic* because it plays out according to the eternal and natural laws of the market: neoliberalism tends to become the realistic religion of today's consumer society, establishing its own gods (the volatile markets that have to be appeased), sacrifices (austerity policies), and commandments (be flexible, adapt, optimize yourself, . . .).[6] Only salvation promises are missing: neoliberalism is a religion without heaven or a final state; and as a *realistic* religion, it regards the journey as its own reward.

Having characterized neoliberalism as a phantom, it might also be true to call it a zombie, as has been increasingly done, for it has obviously not *really* died, although the crash of 2008 irrevocably shattered its ideological foundations. Despite the crashes and catastrophes the neoliberal *casino capitalism* has been kept alive because "there are no alternatives" (too big to fail), because "markets have to be appeased," or simply because this is what "markets require." The *Strange Non-Death of Neoliberalism*, as Colin Crouch has called it,[7] may be explained by the enormous influence of multinational companies on national politics (as Crouch is suggesting), but it also points to the very nature of neoliberalism itself as being much more a path than a goal, as mentioned above, and much more a process than a stable system (so it would be more appropriate to speak of *neoliberalization* than of neoliberalism as such).[8] This projective character—together with its religious realism and also the pecuniary interests of big trusts—helps neoliberalism to stay alive and to continuously remodel our lives, our societies, and our cities.

If this is right, and we assume that the built environment both expresses and shapes social processes, then there must be a profound relationship between neoliberalism and the architecture of our time. But what relationship is it? And how to approach and explain it, especially if we already encounter serious difficulties when trying to explain neoliberalism?

---

[5]   See Foucault, *Birth of Biopolitics*, pp. 228–30.
[6]   On this appellative character of neoliberalism, see Ulrich Bröckling, *Das unternehmerische Selbst: Soziologie einer Subjektivierungsform* (Frankfurt am Main: Suhrkamp, 2007), pp. 46–47.
[7]   Colin Crouch, *The Strange Non-Death of Neoliberalism* (Cambridge: Polity Press, 2011).
[8]   On this topic see, for example, Neil Brenner, Jamie Peck, and Nik Theodore, *Civic City Cahier 4: Afterlives of Neoliberalism* (London: Bedford Press, 2011).

In the last three decades, the impact of the neoliberal restructuring of urban processes has been extensively theorized,[9] but nearly no theorist has tried to pose the question of neoliberalism and architecture as such. In truth, this question is a *tricky* one—and there are plenty of potential objections to it. The first problematic point arises from the difficulty exposed above of deploying the term *neoliberalism* in a precise and substantial way. This difficulty increases even further when the focus is moved from urbanization to individual architectural objects: if certain political and economic processes affecting the built environment at the scale of the city can be (with a sufficient degree of scientific rigor) considered *neoliberal*, then claiming the same for single buildings is much more problematic. Given the capacity of capitalism to absorb and actively (re)produce cultural difference, it is highly questionable if any common aesthetic characteristics can be traced within contemporary global architectural production and identified as exclusively neoliberal.

Another possibility for approaching *neoliberal architecture* would be to explore how the urban policies associated with neoliberalism are brought forward through a set of single architectural interventions. However, a potential difficulty arises from the fact that such interventions are mostly part of broader architectural politics and strategies, so that they cannot be properly understood, if observed separately from the latter.

Further possible approaches would address the question of how the neoliberal doctrine has penetrated architectural discourse and architectural politics; ask how the very concept of architecture—as a form of agency—has been changing under the influence of the neoliberal ideology; explore the emerging associations and dissociations between architecture and other disciplines, which result from the neoliberal restructuring of the spheres of production, consumption, education, and labor; and so forth.

Each of these approaches is potentially problematic and tricky in its own way. But why not interpret the difficulties as challenges and be brave enough to pose the question? Indeed, we should do so if architectural theory aspires to provide a meaningful contextualization of its subject mater in our common and undeniable *neoliberal* reality. Of course, due to the ambiguity and complexity of both sides of the equation, any attempt at formulating an all-embracing meta-theory of architecture and neoliberalism would be misleading. Therefore, the only way to adequately address this question is to examine it from a broad range of perspectives, which link different aspects of neoliberalism to different concepts, components, tendencies, and niches of architecture. So we might conclude: *there is no neoliberal architecture, but there are neoliberal architectures.*

[9]   See, for example, *Urban Asymmetries: Studies and Projects on Neo-
        liberal Urbanization*, eds. Tahl Kaminer, Miguel Robles-Durán, and Heidi
        Sohn (Rotterdam: 010 Publishers, 2011).

In the spring of 2011, we announced a call for papers for an international conference at the Institute for Architectural Theory, Art History and Cultural Studies at Graz University of Technology, to be held at the end of the year to discuss the relationship between architecture and neoliberalism for the first time in a comprehensive and multifaceted way. With the aforementioned difficulties in mind, we gave the title the form of a question: Is there (anti-)neoliberal architecture? The "anti" was posed to also provoke contributions in search of alternatives to the all-encompassing paradigm, which were aimed to counteract the diverse socioeconomic processes associated with neoliberalism. The main goal of our symposium was to redirect the focus of the recent debate on architecture and neoliberalism from the concerns borrowed from urban sociology, human geography, and social anthropology toward the questions belonging more strictly to the thematic field of architectural theory.

Over fifty colleagues from Europe and the US responded to our call and submitted proposals, making it rather difficult to select a few for a two-day conference. In the end, we invited thirteen contributors from very different fields of interest and specialty in order to represent the complexity of our topic. The remarkable conference, which took place in Graz on November 11 and 12, 2011, provoked many discussions and opened up a new field of study in architectural theory. The proceedings at hand, which contain ten of the papers, can be regarded as a first step into this area of research, which will hopefully be followed by further investigations and publications.

Our book is divided into three general chapters. The first deals with the "Historical Origins and Perspectives" of neoliberalization in the nineteen-sixties and seventies and its alternatives in architecture, and is introduced by Ole W. Fischer's essay "From Solid Bodies to Liquid Space." Fisher offers a comprehensive historical review of the origins of neoliberalism and its relationship to architecture till today, beginning with postmodernism which is regarded as "the cultural symptom" of neoliberal capitalism and ending with petrification of architecture after 9/11. Andreas Rumpfhuber likewise locates the neoliberalization of architecture in the nineteen-sixties, but he provides an in-depth study of one special typology: the office landscape. His article "Framing the Possible" focuses on the intertwining of cybernetics with the overall transformation of the working environment and the development of new forms of governance. Tahl Kaminer's paper "In Search of Architectural Efficacy" refers to Henri Lefebvre's analysis of the role of architecture at the University of Nanterre in the students' remonstrations of 1968. Although Kaminer's analysis is rather pessimistic regarding the possibilities of architecture as a *revolutionary* agent, it opens up an interesting perspective on a genuinely architectural contribution to the *reformist* strategies of anti-capitalist politics.

The second, more theoretical chapter discusses "The End (and Return?) of Utopia and Critique" as caused by the neoliberal paradigm.

In "Neoliberalism and the Crisis of the Project," Ana Jeinić relates neoliberalism to the general crisis of *projective thinking* after the discrediting of super-projects like socialism, modernism, and techno-scientism. In her analysis, the different notions of the (non-)project deployed in contemporary architecture are used as models for reflecting on the political strategies of dealing with this alarming situation. Rixt Hoekstra's essay "Neoliberalism and the Possibility of Critique" explains the genesis and portrays the contemporary status quo of (post)critical thinking in architectural practice and the discourses related to it. The text concludes with the appeal to architects to once again understand their practice as a form of intellectual and critical engagement.

The third and largest chapter collects five different "Case Studies" of (anti-)neoliberal discourse, phenomena, and practice in (predominantly contemporary) architecture and design. Maria S. Giudici's "Cautionary Tales" teach us that the futuristic scenarios of Cedric Price, Superstudio, and Archizoom have become reality in the context of neoliberal urbanization. This disconcerting reality has been the subject of a design studio in Athens co-conducted by Giudici, which uncovered the political/economic processes that shape the neoliberal city, while simultaneously encouraging new forms of social interaction. Gideon Boie's essay "Architectural Asymmetries" describes the projects of single-family homes in Antwerp that have been recently developed with the aim of improving the quality of the living environment, while simultaneously fostering city marketing through architecture. The relationship between these projects and neoliberal policies is as ambiguous as neoliberalism itself, as Boie suggests. The last three texts are devoted to individual phenomena that reveal a neoliberal background. In Ana Llorente's "Neoliberal Liaisons," for instance, the remarkable connections between contemporary architecture and fashion are interpreted as symptoms of neoliberal conditions, which tend to celebrate the nomadism, flexibility, and mobility that are exemplarily thematized and preformed in fashion design. Olaf Pfeifer likewise starts his essay "White as the Color of Neoliberalism" with a thorough observation of a fashionable topic: realizing that white has become *the* color of recent decades, Pfeifer demonstrates how the use of white can support the commodification of objects, including architecture. And in "Baukulturindustrie," Oliver Ziegenhardt gives an excellent analysis of a hegemonic discourse that tries to implement neoliberal *Vitalpolitik* into architecture and presents itself as something all-encompassing, compelling, and without alternative.

Finally, we would like to thank all contributors for the wonderful collaboration, as well as Dawn Michelle d'Atri, who did a great job copyediting the whole book, Susanne Rösler, Toni Levak, and Ramona Winkler, who gave it a perfect appearance, and last but not least, the rectorate of Graz University of Technology for kindly making possible the printing of these proceedings.

I.
HISTORICAL ORIGINS
AND PERSPECTIVES

Ole W. Fischer

FROM LIQUID SPACE TO SOLID BODIES
Architecture between Neoliberalism and Control Society

On Form and Content: Architecture with/against Politics?

Traditionally, architecture has been characterized by solidity, structure, and tectonics, that is, by the abstract logic and visual appearance of carry and load. Therefore, we can recognize the metaphor of architecture, the architectonic, or similar terms such as structure or system—in various fields ranging from philosophy, music, and biology to social and political studies—as synonymous with order, logic, organization, and construction. Hence, the suspicion of Jacques Derrida that architecture would be one of the last shelters of metaphysics has its merit.[1] With the advent of the modern project in architecture, however, a new aesthetic questioned the former notion of architectural solidity. With an interest in elevated, hovering volumes and mobile elements, thereby suppressing traditional materiality in favor of the new possibilities of thin constructions and large spans, many modern architectural designs employed abstracted elements (line, plane, volume), breaking up the traditional boxed spaces in order to enable a transition between inside and out. Structure obtained new meaning as architects, influenced by Zeitgeist theories, looked into function, machine aesthetics, and new technologies as a translation of industrial society and enlightenment rationalism, but also as means for shaping a new society. Even if the relationship between modern architecture and politics

[1] Jacques Derrida, "Point de Folie: Maintenant l'architecture," in Bernard Tschumi, *La Case Vide: La Villete, 1985* (London: Architectural Association, 1986).

is unstable—ranging from bourgeois aestheticism and apolitical technocracy to social-democratic reform and revolutionary stances (in both fascist and communist *couleur*)—the utopian aspect of transforming society with design was widely accepted.

Exactly this compliance of modern architecture (and more so: urbanism) with vanguard politics has been under the attack since the nineteen-sixties, with critics claiming the futility, if not arrogance, of architects in thinking that they could change society. The formal break with the modernist aesthetics of abstraction, reduction, and functional industrial design has been presented as *liberation* from the design orthodoxies of a so-called elitist, academic, and hegemonic modernism. Questioning the modern collective narratives of *progress*, *new man*, and *new society*, the protagonists of what later would be called *postmodernism* proposed individualism, pluralism, consumerism, aestheticism, irony, and identity politics with historical, pop, and vernacular references. In addition, many ushered environmental, social, and behavioral concerns, while, last but not least, some raised a severe neo-Marxist, structuralist, and poststructuralist critique of modernity and its visual representation in the built environment. If postmodern architects seem(ed) to be obsessed with the question of meaning in architecture—ranging from images, ornament, history, context, and typology to semiotics or syntactics—there was an intentional distancing from politics. Even outspoken political architects such as Aldo Rossi (a member of the Partito Comunista Italiano, Italy's communist party) famously stated the following in his inaugural lecture at the Swiss Federal Institute of Technology Zurich (ETH) in 1972, in reaction to the student protests of 1968: "The instruments of the architect are pencil, ruler and compass." And the neo-Marxist architectural historian Manfredo Tafuri announced the end of the modern utopian project and argued—under the circumstances of advanced capitalism—for a separation of criticism from design practice.

Yet, is it possible to disconnect architecture from political implications and social contents, or shall we think of the willful disassociation, apolitical idleness, and ironic distancing of the postmodern stance as a hidden political project? Several authors such Fredric Jameson,[2] David Harvey,[3] and, more recently, Reinhold Martin[4] have argued for the latter, that postmodernism in its various incarnations (from neo-historicism, contextualism, typology, regionalism, and playful figurativeness to high-tech, neo-modern, and deconstruction) is the cultural symptom or the representation of neoliberal capitalism.

---

[2]   Fredric Jameson, *Postmodernism, or, The Cultural Logic of Late Capitalism* (Durham: Duke University Press, 1991).
[3]   David Harvey, *The Condition of Postmodernity: An Enquiry into the Origins of Cultural Change* (Oxford and Cambridge, MA: Blackwell, 1990).
[4]   Reinhold Martin, *Utopia's Ghost: Architecture and Postmodernism, again* (Minneapolis: University of Minnesota Press, 2010).

Because of its all-encompassing, prominent, and impure character, architecture and urban space are as much a product as they are a subject of societies—such as that of authors and authorities, of clients, collaborators, and connoisseurs, of users, neighbors, and passersby, or of the general public—which renders the built environment as a primary site for taking stock of the present cultural condition. Architectural form forms behaviors, as it is informed by political, economic, and sociocultural circumstances. From this perspective, built environments, forms of spatial appropriation, and designs of high public interest, media coverage, and emotional debate can serve as a reflection of the desires, discourses, and ideologies of their time. In other words, architecture can be thought of as an expression of an era, with its aesthetics negotiating the ethics of the time, very much like the Zeitgeist protagonists of the modern project wanted it to be. Yet these protagonists imagined that architecture would present itself as linear, voluntary, and outspoken commentary on the present, or even as a heroic utopian cue to the future, whereas today, architecture seems more like a residue or secretion of the society that brought it about (in the sense of Henri Lefebvre). Buildings and urban spaces—both everyday generic ones and authored, outstanding singular pieces—can be identified and grouped because they imbed the preferences and sensibilities of a specific time period and cultural climate. Architecture speaks, whether willfully or by accident, of the projections, dreams, and wishes of a time, of the tastes and emotions, as much as of the sociopolitical history or the history of ideas (what Fredric Jameson calls its "symptomatology").[5] The immersion of architecture into the capitalist reality of society, economy, and culture—very much like product design, advertising, fashion, or film—may shed light on the paradox that architecture today seems to represent contemporary culture by avoiding the present.

Architecture and Neoliberalism: A Brief History

Yet what do we mean by neoliberalism? Originally phrased in the nineteen-thirties—as an alternative to the laissez-faire liberalism of the nineteenth and early twentieth centuries—to sustain a democratic liberal market society with some state control so as to prevent another crash, a great depression, and social unrest (ordo-liberalism), today it describes a society that subsumes all human relations under the frame of the market. With the words of Harvey: "Neoliberalism is in the first instance a theory of political economic practices that proposes that human well-being can best be advanced by liberating

[5]   Fredric Jameson, "Symptoms of Theory or Symptoms for Theory?," *Critical Inquiry* 30, no. 2 (Winter 2004), pp. 403–8.

individual entrepreneurial freedoms and skills within an institutional framework characterized by strong private property rights, free markets, and free trade."[6]

This definition puts neoliberalism in dialectic opposition to Keynesianism, that is, to the post-Depression and postwar welfare state and the demand-driven economics that targeted problems of capitalist distribution and malfunction of the market with interventionist politics. The twist of neoliberalism lies in the equation of economic freedom (individual entrepreneurial freedom and property rights) with political freedom, or rather, in the condemnation of state intervention into economic and private life as collective totalitarianism that would lead directly to socialism or fascism.[7] Instead, neoliberalism demands deregulation, liberalization (labor market, trade, tariffs), floating exchange rates, privatization and withdrawal of the state,[8] flat taxes, reduction of public spending (respectively deficits), et cetera, since its theorists model the market as fully transparent, as a sum of individual economic decisions (microeconomics), and as capable of the best distribution of goods and services that would allow for individual freedom of choice, a sense of responsibility, and self-fulfillment. Harvey shows how this reevaluation of classic liberalist market theories, with the related ideology of rendering all human relations in economic terms, serves class interests and how it moved from a minority position (postwar) to academic and political hegemony (after 1989) since it presented itself as successful, realistic, pragmatic, and "without alternative."

Against the foil of neoliberalism, the rise of postmodern architecture seems no coincidence: there is a strong chronological parallel of both being a latent discourse in the nineteen-sixties, their rise during the seventies, and their hegemony in the eighties and nineties, for there are resonances in content and rhetoric. Postmodern theorists have claimed freedom of choice in terms of lifestyle, embraced pop culture, media, and tradition, addressed individualism, pluralism, and differentiation, and sported an aversion to standardization, collective movements (like CIAM), but also to urbanism and planning, featuring instead the singular architectural object invested in the production of meaning. The crisis of the object and the predicament of (urban) tex-

[6]   David Harvey, *Brief History of Neoliberalism* (Oxford: Oxford University Press, 2005), p. 2.
[7]   These are the words of Friedrich August von Hayek and Milton Friedman, but what about Pinochet's Chile or Deng's China? See: Hayek, *The Road of Serfdom* (London: Routledge, 1944); see: Friedman, *Capitalism and Freedom* (Chicago: University of Chicago Press, 1962).
[8]   The role of the state is twofold (and contradictory), since the state should refrain from intervention and not interfere with the "wisdom" of the market, but on the other hand the state needs to be strong enough to enforce law, property rights, monetary stability, and to resolve market imbalances (monopoly).

ture, to use the words of Colin Rowe,[9] have been one of the main points of critique against CIAM urban planning (→**1**, →**2**). However the dissolution of the city and the evaporation of public space have continued, if not intensified, over the past decades. Exceptions, such as the IBA Berlin or the transformation of Barcelona, became possible by *old school* strong municipalities and government interventions into the housing market. But with the appreciation of Charles Moore for Disneyland,[10] or of Robert Venturi and Denise Scott-Brown for the US commercial strip, the conventional suburban house, and the *democratic* entertainment of Las Vegas enjoyed from the car,[11] the connection to the neoliberal ideology of individualism and the market becomes clear. The disintegration of the city into historic cores restored for touristic display, iconic buildings, hotel complexes, shopping malls and big-box retail, edge cities with office parks, entertainment parks, suburbia and gated communities—all these features follow the logic of differentiation, privatization, individualization, customization, and commodification or, in short, of market logic.

Here, the model of the entertainment park is especially revealing: Rem Koolhaas has suggested a reading of Coney Island as a laboratory for the urbanization of Manhattan. In his "retroactive manifesto" of 1978,[12] Koolhaas critiqued the intentional political utopianism of the European avant-gardes with an alternative narration of the "blind" evolution of multiple metropolitan lifestyles fired by capitalist speculation, technological advancement, and irrational human desires. And it was not for nothing that he played out the dualism between Le Corbusier and Salvador Dalí, opting for the latter and his paranoiac-critical method (despite the doubts expressed by other Surrealists about Dalí's relationship to Franco and the Catholic Church). If Tafuri believed that modern architecture came close to its political potential of changing society with the (urban) plan in Le Corbusier's *Plan Obus* for Algiers of 1933, Koolhaas makes the counterargument that Le Corbusier borrowed his urban ideas from Manhattan but stripped the model of all its qualities—mainly the density, contradiction, and artificiality of the "culture of congestion" and delivered rational banality instead of surreal experimentation. The Manhattan of the early twentieth century, in the rear mirror of Koolhaas, offers a different lesson:

[9]   Colin Rowe and Fred Koetter, *Collage City* (Cambridge, MA: MIT Press, 1978).
[10]   Charles Moore, "You Have to Pay for the Public Life," *Perspecta* 9–10 (1965), pp. 57–97, here p. 65.
[11]   Robert Venturi, Denise Scott Brown, and Steven Izenour, *Learning from Las Vegas* (Cambridge, MA: MIT Press, 1972); 2nd edition: *Learning from Las Vegas: The Forgotten Symbolism of Architectural Form* (Cambridge, MA: MIT Press, 1977).
[12]   Rem Koolhaas, *Delirious New York: A Retroactive Manifesto for Manhattan* (Oxford and New York: Oxford University Press, 1978; new edition: New York: Monacelli, 1994).

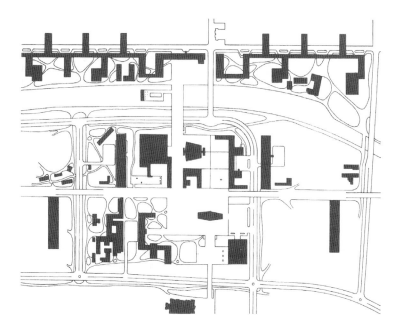

(1) Le Corbusier, Project for Saint-Dié, Figure-Ground Plan, 1945
Source: Colin Rowe and Fred Koetter, *Collage City* (Cambridge: MIT Press,1978), p. 62

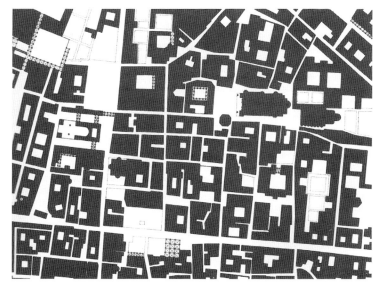

(2) Parma, Figure-Ground Plan
Source: Colin Rowe and Fred Koetter, *Collage City* (Cambridge: MIT Press,1978), p. 63

the combination of (potentially limitless) street grids and urban blocks filled with tripartite skyscrapers (base, shaft, corona) enables a virtually endless stacking of alternative lifestyles that are only connected by circulation (elevator) and common envelope (Skyscraper Theorem,[13]

[13]   Ibid., pp. 82–85.

(3) Rem Koolhaas, *The Skyscraper Theorem* taken from Life, 1909
Source: Rem Koolhaas, *Delirious New York* (Oxford: Oxford University Press, 1978), p.69

Downtown Athletic Club[14]) (→**3**,→**4**). The large urban building potentially houses a variety of programs and entertains radical, contradicting human behaviors in a series of artificial environments that do not
register at the outside (in difference again to Le Corbusier's modernist
belief in the *truth* of showing structure, material, and use). Koolhaas
dubbed this disconnect of the individual on the inside from the urban
(or collective) appearance on the outside "lobotomy" with reference
to the acquainted neurosurgical procedure of cutting the connection to the prefrontal cortex. With other words metaphorically taken
again from medicine, the schizophrenic split between the large urban
form and its contained pluralism of interior worlds—which Koolhaas

[14]   Ibid., pp. 152–59.

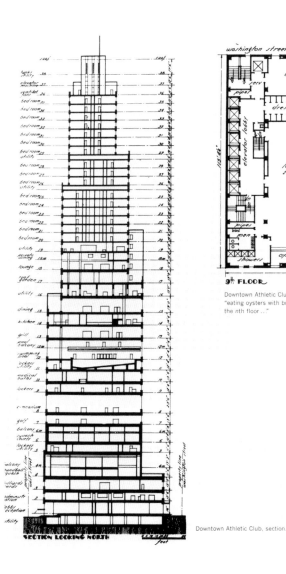

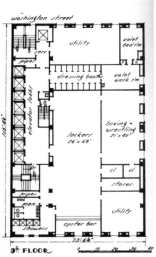

(4) Starrett & Van Vleck, Downtown Athletic Club, New York, 1931
Source: Rem Koolhaas, *Delirious New York* (Oxford: Oxford University Press, 1978), p.128

Downtown Athletic Club, plan of ninth floor: "eating oysters with boxing gloves, naked, on the *n*th floor ..."

Downtown Athletic Club, section.

labeled as "Bigness" in his seminal book *S,M,L,XL* of 1995[15] and which is at the center of Jameson's critique of the postmodern interiors of John Portman's hotel complexes—was already present in *Delirious New York* of 1978. Here architecture replaces the city, and the large building sucks in the multiplicity of program and people of the metropolitan public spaces, up to the point that it no longer needs the city grid but becomes an autonomous fact in itself, dependent only

[15]   Rem Koolhaas and Bruce Mau, *Small, Medium, Large, Extra-Large: Office for Metropolitan Architecture*, ed. Jennifer Sigler (New York: Monacelli Press, 1995); here: "Bigness or The Problem of Large," pp. 494–516.

(5) Madelon Vriesendorp, *The City of the Captive Globe,* 1972
Source: Rem Koolhaas, *Delirious New York* (Oxford: Oxford University Press, 1978), p. 142

(6) Charles Jencks, *Evolutionary Tree to the Year 2000*
Source: idem, *Architecture 2000: Predictions and Methods* (London: Studio Vista, 1971), p. 46–7

(7) Charles Jencks, *Evolutionary Tree 20th Century Architecture*
Source: idem, *Architecture 2000: Predictions and Methods* (London: Wiley, 2000), p. 4–5

on infrastructure. In the appendix of *Delirious New York*, Koolhaas already presents an idealized architectural representation of neoliberal society and global economy: *The City of the Captive Globe* (→**5**), of which he writes: "It is the capital of Ego, where science, art, poetry and forms of madness compete under ideal conditions to invent, destroy and restore the world of phenomenal Reality. Each Science or Mania has its own plot. . . . The changes in this ideological skyline will be rapid and continuous: a rich spectacle of ethical joy, moral fever or intellectual masturbation."[16]

Like the speculative evolutionary pool of architectural styles drawn by Charles Jencks in 1971 (and revised in 2001) (→**6**,→**7**), Koolhaas offers a free choice of ideological, formal, and social constructs represented by the multiplicity of design attitudes. Each of those might be radical in its own stand, yet as an ensemble they turn into samples, into available lifestyles on the market (note: "compete" in the quote), where, by the very means of their massing, they annihilate each other in their transformative, utopian power. And again, like Jencks, the most important feature of this concept model often goes unrecognized: the line around the evolutionary tree, or rather, the frame of grid and base. The line allows only for a recombination of the existing styles and prevents new *species* from arising, while the grid is potentially endless, therefore the choice of *radical* alternatives, which are orderly stowed like the umpteen different toothpastes in the supermarket that evoke freedom of choice for the consumer, while any true alternative—revolutionary practice instead of evolutionary recombination of the always

[16]   Koolhaas, *Delirious New York*, p. 294.

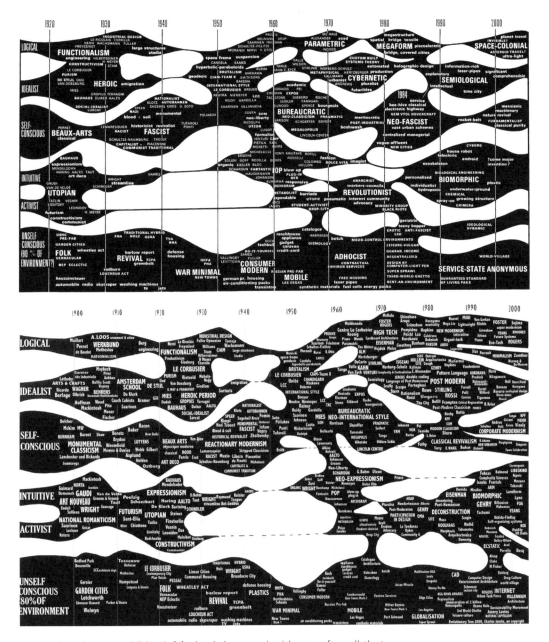

same—has been prohibited. Maybe it is no coincidence after all that *Delirious New York* was published in 1978—in chronological proximity to Margaret Thatcher, Deng Xiaoping's opening of China, and the presidency of Ronald Reagan?[17]

[17]   See Harvey, *Brief History of Neoliberalism*, p. 1.

Liquidity: Architecture and Globalization

If one speaks today of architecture and globalization, it is almost a given to refer to Frank Gehry and the Guggenheim Museum Bilbao (1997) as a paradigmatic example of *neoliberal* or *globalized* design and the celebrity system of starchitecture. Much has been written about the expansive strategy of the Guggenheim Foundation under the director Thomas Krens, the signature sculptural approach of Gehry as exemplifying new digital construction methods for a truly spectacular building, the press campaign, and the worldwide reception of the museum. All of the above brought the economically worn-out, postindustrial Basque harbor city onto the cosmopolitan map of tourism and created both jobs and revenue: the so-called *Bilbao effect* (→**8**). However, what often goes unrecognized is the fact that a public client commissioned the museum. This pattern is typical of starchitecture—public clients, often cultural institutions, are responsible for a good share of the iconic buildings of the nineteen-nineties and two-thousands. What might look like a counterargument to neoliberalism—since, following the hypothesis of the retreat of the state and the domination of private interests, one would expect to find mainly private and corporate clients[18]—makes sense against the background of a neoliberal reorganization of the state, especially in the cultural and educational sectors. Here, a severe competition for public legitimization in the form of memberships, visitors, press coverage, donors, or public and private attention has changed the institutional landscape dramatically. While public funding became less reliable over the years due to budget cuts in the municipalities and states, cultural institutions were targeted as the main infrastructures for tourism and city marketing. Following the logic of neoliberalism, cities, regions, and states came to understand themselves as competitors on a global market—competitors for tourists, but also for human resources attracted by cultural capital. The renaissance of metropolitan areas such as London, New York, or Berlin has much to do with this, and one side effect is gentrification. A second factor in this connection between public institutions and iconic buildings under the logic of neoliberalism is the transformation of the organizations themselves: their personnel tends toward global networks and contexts, which influences the setting of institutional goals and decision-making processes, while favoring internationally acclaimed *brands* of starchitects. A market of attention results in a certain *festivalization* of institutions and entire cities, which means a shift toward one-time project funding instead of annual subsidies, with new buildings or spectacular extensions as

[18]   For an account of corporate architecture, see Anna Klingmann, *Brandscapes: Architecture in the Experience Economy* (Cambridge, MA: MIT Press, 2007).

one of the main features (often the big name of the starchitect helps to allocate public support, but also to ensure private donations in the time of decreasing state funding). This comes as a surprise, if one considers the potential risks resulting from commissions to *experimental* designs and vanguard technologies, such as malfunctioning buildings, delays, and an increase in construction costs, especially for public clients.[19]

Yet none of this has answered the question of formal qualities, or the direction of international architecture in the nineteen-nineties and two-thousands. Compared to earlier, collaged, postmodernist, iconic buildings citing historic references (or Pop Art) and the first generation of deconstructivist designs of the eighties, which featured disintegrated, deformed, and reiterated elements, fragmented pieces, sliced and bent structures, superimposed layers and interfered orders, displacement, collisions and traces of forces—in short, a questioning of traditional design values—a new aesthetic gained ground in the nineties: collage and fragmentation were replaced by continuous, seamless surfaces, by merged volumes and transient flows. Also here, the Guggenheim Museum Bilbao marks an important threshold: while it still features certain characteristics of the earlier *deconstructivism*, like the sliced surfaces and abrupt changes of materials (→**9**), the paneling of titan sheet metal on a steel frame where each element is custom-made has become possible with CAD and digital fabrication (→**10**). But it would be too deterministic to reduce the preference of liquid analogies, of streams, curves, channels, and currents, only to the new digital technologies of image creation, drawing, modeling, and production techniques. Concepts like hybridization, grafting, merging, and morphing indicate more than CAD and Photoshop: they speak of a fascination of architects with the liquefaction of space, the

[19]   This might recall the current struggle around the *Elbphilharmonie* in
         Hamburg by Herzog & de Meuron.

(9) Frank O. Gehry, Guggenheim
Museum Bilbao, 1993–97, detail

compression of time to an instant presence due to electronic real-
time transfers, and the dematerialization in a mediatized age. And
they indicate the challenge to human self-perception and our concept
of nature (similar to Darwin in the nineteenth century) after the decoding of genetic information opened the door to genetic manipulation:
the virtual suddenly seemed to be more real. If manufacturing and
production in postindustrial society can be said to have lost their value
(compared to modern architecture), then the collection, management,
manipulation, and visualization of data have promised the discovery of
a new continent, of a transgressive force similar to the discovery of
the Americas in the Renaissance. Yet all these hopes and phantasies
belong more to phantasmagoria, that is, simulacra: like Columbus,
who thought he had discovered the passage to India, the virtual world
is the other side of borderless and limitless streams of capital, goods,
people, and information or, in short, of globalization and neoliberal
politics[20] (→**11**). The promise of more direct interaction with other
people (ideally, the whole world population) and of Internet-based direct democracy is only the flip side of a network that grew out of
the Cold War military-industrial complex (which today would be more
aptly called the *military-industrial-organizational complex*). It serves
mainly to move data and capital around the globe in real time and has
quickly been absorbed as the ideal global marketplace. The promise
of computer-based statistics to manage large data packages and to
represent the invisible information graphically soon had to be given
up, as did the promise of actually controlling these forces, such as

[20]   Again I refer to David Harvey, who pointed out the close connection
        between de-industrialization in the West, the transfer of work to a
        global market, and the need for IT to organize the flows. See Harvey,
        Brief History of Neoliberalism, pp. 3–4, 34, and 157–59.

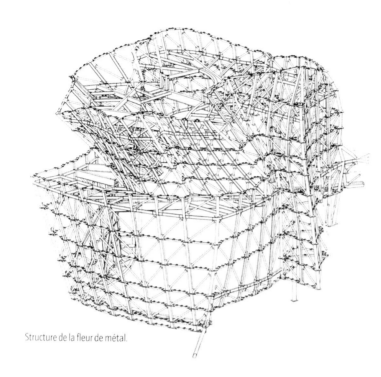

(10) Frank O. Gehry, Guggenheim Museum Bilbao, 1996, CAD drawing of the steel structure

Structure de la fleur de métal.

the weather models, traffic models, or software for stock-market analysis that took control of the global flow of (virtual) capital. From this perspective, the notion of *critical architecture*, which has been introduced as another label for deconstructivist trends, does not go without irony: the offices prominently displayed in the MoMA show of 1988[21]—Frank Gehry, Peter Eisenman, Coop Himmelb(l)au, Rem Koolhaas/OMA, Zaha Hadid, Bernard Tschumi, and Daniel Libeskind—read today like the *who's who* of starchitecture.

What Ever Happened to Architecture after 9/11?

If the paradigm of liquid space that was already latently present in modern architecture fully unfolded in nineteen-nineties in parallel to the fall of the Berlin Wall, which turned the Western neoliberal model into a truly global practice—with strong backlashes on the Western developed world—and if the idea of emergence, morphing, and design evolution outside of the traditional formal vocabulary of architecture can be traced to both genetics and the IT revolution, then what is the state of affairs today?

[21]   Philip Johnson and Mark Wigley, *Deconstructivist Architecture* (New York: Museum of Modern Art, 1988).

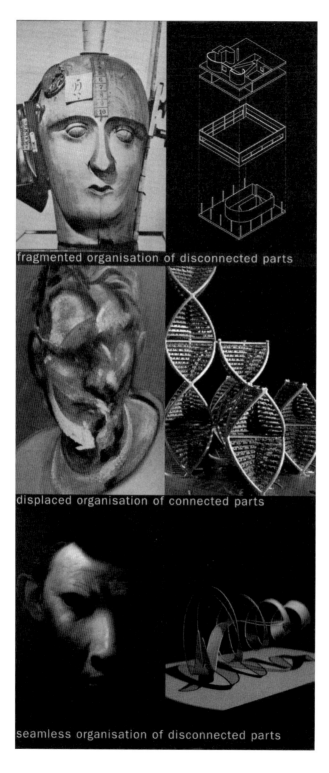

(11) UNStudio (Ben van Berkel),
Diagram
Source: Ben van Berkel and Caroline Bos, *Techniques,* Move vol. 2
(Amsterdam: UN Studio, 1999), p. 85

fragmented organisation of disconnected parts

displaced organisation of connected parts

seamless organisation of disconnected parts

Deconstructivist formal tendencies are still in high fashion, though often updated to parametric design and landscape urbanism (a flow that undermines the borders between animate and inanimate materials). However, there is an oppositional trend toward a rematerialization of the delineation of space: articulated thresholds, the growing complexity and thickness of envelopes, and an increased focus on structure demonstrate a general hardening of surfaces, a petrification of architectural borders. There are two potential reasons for this: security and sustainability. The first has to do with post-9/11 trauma: architecture is under attack. The drama around the rebuilding of Ground Zero, where the sign of a victorious America envisioned by Libeskind as the Freedom Tower—rising 1,776 feet (541 meters) into the air—turned into a massive windowless bunker-base of sixty meters, is only the most obvious example (→**12**). Of course, human catastrophes have always been written into the building codes (regarding structural integrity, earthquakes, fires, or even atomic war), but since 2001, Western societies have started to view architecture and urban space predominantly from the *state of exception* perspective: the performance of design in case of assault, terror, or panic. The notion of smooth space and frictionless flow (with a nod to Deleuze and Guattari) has been replaced by active and passive defense—that is, shock resistance and surveillance, leading to a control society (Foucault). Yet to speak here of a return to the *strong state* would be premature, since, as Harvey has pointed out,[22] the success of neoliberal politics since the eighties has been closely connected to wars: the Cold War, the Falklands War, the Persian Gulf wars, and finally the Global War against Terror with its main theater of Iraq. Despite the theory of neoliberalism, which links economic freedom to political and individual liberation, the practice of neoliberally informed governments seems to move in the opposite direction: toward replacing democratic politics and consensual government with authoritarian governance and control society.

Sustainability is a more complicated issue: neoliberalism in theory and practice has resisted any form of environmental standards and state control mechanisms as a form of state intervention into the market, preferring to ignore the externalized costs for air, water, land, biodiversity, and human health, up to the point of questioning the statistics and models of the international scientific community on human-induced climate change. Today, there seems to be a change of strategy: if there should be any consideration of external costs, neoliberal protagonists argue, then they must follow market mechanisms, such as for instance emission trading (for CO_2). And while continental European governments have determined standards for energy efficiency and sustainability, the Anglo-Saxon world follows a different model of nongovernmental institutions promoting *sustainable* design, like the Green Building Council, a non-profit NGO, which succeeded in establishing its Leadership in Energy and Environmental Design (LEED) certificate as a voluntary industrial standard in the building sector.

While a few years ago architects worried that the material of architecture would "evaporate" due to new technologies of building control, the material sciences, and nomadic patterns of behavior—something that Reyner Banham and Archigram were already embracing in the

---

[22]   Harvey, *Brief History of Neoliberalism*, pp. 6–7 and 79ff.

sixties[23]—we are now witnessing the opposite effect: densification and thickness, especially on the exterior-interior threshold. If the regime of security asks for identification, surveillance, and control of the global streams of people, goods, and capital, then the regime of sustainability enforces a system of controlled metabolism, or flows of materials, people, and especially energy.

The establishment of standards—voluntary or by intervention of the state—is, however, only the technical side of *green building*; so far architects have rarely integrated these technologies and transformed them into themes of design. Parameters like site, connection to public space and public transport, orientation, volumetry, typologies, envelope, materials and their heat transfer coefficient, and climate technology with water, waste, and energy management have been delegated to specialists and computer programs, instead of being turned into a new *material* of architecture—such as modernism worked through the new industrial basis of society as an architectural program. Or shall we read the renaissance of two already widely criticized and debunked architectural styles as advent of the new green architecture to come? Since in the United States both *new urbanism* (with its battle cry for the small city of traditional urban morphology, pedestrianism, local materials, and building practice) and *critical regionalism* (with a similar, though more phenomenological, approach to place, type, local building practice, and materiality) have recently claimed ownership of *sustainable*, *green*, or *ecological architecture*. True, in history one can frequently witness a return to traditional patterns, if not to straight classicism, as a reaction to social crises. But I hope that neo-historicism, regionalism, or new urbanism is not the final answer.

[23]   See Reyner Banham, *The Architecture of the Well-Tempered Environment* (London: Architectural Press, 1969); see *Archigram—Magazine for New Ideas in Architecture*, published in London between 1961 and 1970.

Andreas Rumpfhuber

FRAMING THE POSSIBLE
Cybernetic Neoliberalism and the Architecture of Immaterial Labor

Occasionally, architecture frames the emergence of a new collective.[1] In this rare instance, architecture introduces a rhythm to the environment. It might become part of an emancipatory process altering the existing social order. In general terms, architecture supplies an organization of space that constructs possibilities of how to engage with one another; simultaneously, it allows for the insulation of the individual. Yet architecture is amalgamated with what constitutes society. The practice of space production is directly related to and dependent on economic and political discourse, as well as technical advancements. It mirrors and reflects ideas and concepts of how to cope, govern, and design our world by contributing different and yet sometimes unprecedented organizations and framings of space.

For the contemporary practice of space production in Western industrial societies, the nineteen-sixties represent a significant moment—marking the transition from a Fordist mode of predominantly material production toward a post-Fordist labor paradigm in which "immaterial labour"[2] was to become the dominant form of value production. This restructuring process of society was accompanied by the introduction of the thought model of cybernetics and its technical advancement of calculating machines and automats. In these years, cybernetics

[1]   The research for this text was funded by the Austrian Science Fund
        (FWF): P 22447-G21. The material has mostly been taken from my
        recently published book, *Architektur immaterieller Arbeit* (Vienna: Turia
        und Kant, 2012).
[2]   Maurizio Lazzarato, "Immaterial Labour," http://www.generation-online.
        org/c/fcimmateriallabour3.htm (accessed April 2013).

became highly popular across the academic disciplines and was celebrated in lifestyle magazines. It ultimately fostered the utopia of *the end of labor* and its pragmatic implementation: *the leisure society*.

The transition from a Fordist mode of production toward the ever more dominant form of post-Fordism was coupled with an intensification of the economy and its driving discourse and logic, namely: neoliberalism. In fact, neoliberalism reached a new level with the introduction of cybernetics, as stressed, for instance, by Donna Haraway in her cyborg manifesto: "Michael Foucault's biopolitics is a flaccid premonition of cyborg politics."[3] But also anarchist thinkers, like the Tiqqun collective, have aptly pointed out how the new thought model of cybernetics actually heightened and strengthened not only the mode of exploitation but the very (neoliberal) ideology of contemporary capitalism. In other words: the nineteen-sixties and early seventies witnessed a renewed and radicalized idea of how to govern society.

On a concrete and mundane level, this means that approaches to living and working irrevocably changed during the nineteen-sixties. Work time and spare time started to merge, and the actual job became indistinguishable from education and vocational training. Yet these alterations of the capitalist paradigm were of course not limited to the social, political, and economic spheres alone; they also powerfully affected architecture and the built environment. The impact of new modes and means of production on the urban fabric led to the emergence of new and unprecedented spatial figurations. Architects and spatial theorists have noted and described these changes in manifold ways since the sixties; never, however, through the concept of labor. Aside from an increasingly vivid critical discourse in the social sciences, cultural theory, gender studies, and even management studies, popular debate around post-Fordist workplaces and their neoliberal constitution has been framed not by the complex of labor, but by its opposite: leisure, housing, and—on an urban scale—the identitarian politics of corporations and cities.

In the following, I will discuss paradigmatic European projects that occurred more or less simultaneously in the nineteen-sixties. The examples explicate spatially the transition from a Fordist labor paradigm to a post-Fordist mode of production: from a clearly marked space toward a global infrastructure; from a space ordered by a disciplinary form of hierarchy to a generic space containing a networked society with a flat organizational hierarchy; from the passive "organization man" in the office toward the creative and active "entrepreneurial"

[3]   Donna Haraway, "A Cyborg Manifesto: Science, Technology, and
        Socialist-Feminism in the Late Twentieth Century," in *Simians, Cyborgs
        and Women: The Reinvention of Nature* (New York: Routledge, 1991),
        pp. 149–81, esp. pp. 149–50.

self (*Unternehmerisches Selbst*)[4] working, no matter where, in a bubble. I will focus briefly on several projects: the first ever built Büro-landschaft (office landscape), called Buch und Ton (1959–60), for the Bertelsmann corporation by management consultants Eberhard and Wolfgang Schnelle; Cedric Price's Fun Palace (1961–66); and Herman Hertzberger's Centraal Beheer (1968–71). I will then present the Austrian architect Hans Hollein's television performance *Mobile Office* (1969) and Archizoom Associati's No-Stop City (1969). The projects pragmatically engage in a world full of labor, making it possible for me to identify and to analyze the contours of an exemplary architecture, one that mirrors the tendencies of altering modes of production and the labor conditions of a value-adding, immaterial practice in the moment of its emergence.

Partly reactive, partly prophetic (from a present-day perspective), the projects that I discuss deal with two things: firstly, the sheer endless expansion (in terms of both time and space) of workplaces into society; and, secondly, the modes of assembly, the imagination of collective life, and not least the political relevance of the architect's practice in a post-Fordist era under neoliberal governmentality.

Calculation of Bürolandschaft

Setting the scene for my discussion, the project Buch und Ton—the world's very first Bürolandschaft—was designed in 1959 by a transdisciplinary team of German computer and information scientists, mathematicians, and philosophers close to the management consultants Eberhard and Wolfgang Schnelle. Buch und Ton was a test space for the publisher and mail-order company Bertelsmann. It was housed in the converted top floor of an existing warehouse for books and records at the company site, and was roughly half the size of a football pitch. Buch und Ton was an experiment in spatial organization using a cybernetic design method, creating the prototype of the post-Fordist workspace with a flat hierarchy aspiring to a democratic workspace.[5] The design of Buch und Ton followed the logic of a working community with a flat hierarchy consisting of small, manageable groups and teams with no supervisor or group leader, or, alternatively, with the boss positioned as part of the group among his team members. It was the cybernetically calculated arrangement of flexible workspaces and their reciprocal relations, the placement of potted plants and screens,

[4]   Ulrich Bröckling, *Das unternehmerische Selbst: Soziologie einer Subjektivierungsform* (Frankfurt am Main: Suhrkamp, 2007).
[5]   For an elaborate discussion of the Buch und Ton office landscape as the prototype of a control-society space, see Andreas Rumpfhuber, "Space of Information Flow: The Schnelle Brothers' Office Landscape, Buch und Ton," in *Experiments: Architecture between Science and the Arts* (Berlin: Jovis, 2011), pp. 200–25.

(1) Bürolandschaft Buch und Ton,
Bertelsmann, Gütersloh, 1959–61
© Archive Gebrüder Schnelle/
Andreas Rumpfhuber

and even the calculated color choice of the ceiling that allowed the stark and endless interior to become subjectively and visually chaotic and therefore impossible to survey in an old-fashioned, hierarchical way (→**1**). A form of governance, based on cybernetic principles, was already in place in this space, encouraging each of the coworkers to take responsibility for the organization while, in parallel, automats would take over repetitive work processes. As the designers would state, people were freed from repetitive and tedious work processes. At the same time, each of the workers and employees—not yet redundant in the face of technology—were addressed as specialists and assigned a specific function. As the implicit argument goes, until full automation is possible, workers need to actively participate in a team and shoulder responsibility for the corporation.

This organization of work processes, in which calculation machines and automats were implemented into administrative work with the aim of full automation, together with the activation of the autonomous laborer, signified the office landscape's transition into post-Fordist labor conditions and their neoliberal ideals of governance. On the one hand, it dismissed people to be taken care of outside of the factory by social liberalism and the welfare state; on the other, it actually freed them from a fixed space of work, rhetorically upgrading laborers to become specialists, to become researchers, or to become creative. It appealed to them to assume responsibility for the corporation, extending their productivity into even the ample leisure and recreation areas within the office landscape. Ultimately, the system aspired to create a highly flexible, self-organized, democratic society of specialist laborers without clearly assigned management.

The space that housed this cybernetically organized labor society seemed to be extensive—almost endlessly vast. In fact, it was marked by the clear border of the glass walls delimiting the labor organization and holding it within its clearly marked confines (→**2**). Its interior figuration appeared to be irregular, indeed chaotic; nonethe-

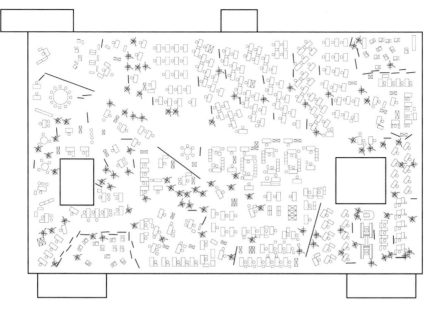

(2) Layout of the Bürolandschaft Buch und Ton, Bertelsmann, Gütersloh, 1959–61, reconstruction by Andreas Rumpfhuber

less, a strict and meticulous order reigned. The space was arranged through a network-like organization of what would ideally be a completely transparent information flow between all actors—be they human or nonhuman—placed in small teams within the space. The relational dependency of the actors in the network of information flows ensured a system that achieved the best possible performance; an arrangement that focused on company profits and whose design was unified, measurable, and verifiable. It was designed as a sealed-in mechanism that is highly flexible in its interior. At the same time, Buch und Ton was only a relay for a much wider and much more expansive space of the similar cybernetically organized Bertelsmann mail-order business. This network-like expansion, which already covered the whole of Germany in the early nineteen-sixties, worked through its continuous feedback loops, permanently optimizing the production-distribution-consumption process.

Spatial *Entgrenzung:* Work Spilling Out into the City

After 1959, the office landscape soon extended its conceptual hold far beyond the controlled office space itself. About ten years later, the Dutch Architect Herman Hertzberger implemented a similar concept in his office building Centraal Beheer (1969–71) in Apeldoorn (→**3**). His structurally open and porous megastructure was the explicit architectonic antithesis to office landscaping. Hertzberger's anti-Bürolandschaft followed a similar form to the organizational pattern of office landscaping and its spatial explication, but it arrived at a strikingly

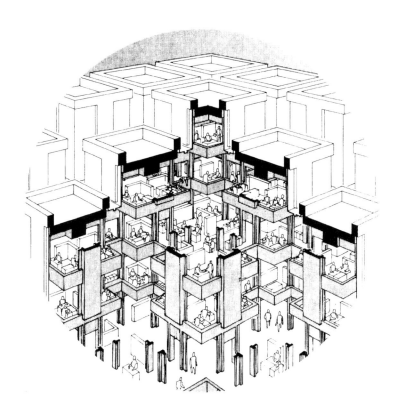

different, three-dimensional spatial solution. Managerially speaking, it was no longer the single instance (the individual human laborer or the machine) but a team of about four members that constituted the smallest spatial and organizational entity for the corporation. In the smallest possible space, a socially ordered group of four organized and introduced a rhythm into the vast open space of Centraal Beheer. Hertzberger conceived of small stackable units, so-called islands, allowing for a multitude of administrative work situations: the single or group work space; the conference room; the café; the restaurant; and also spaces for informal meetings in between. The formerly horizontal and homogenous space of the office landscape was now established by islands stacked three-dimensionally.

Conceptionally speaking, Hertzberger's architecture is like the generic space of the Bürolandschaft: an utterly neutral container that functions as infrastructure, and which allows the user to actively adapt the architecture to any use (→**4**). With his concept of polyvalency, however, Hertzberger delineated a flexible, somehow emancipated spatial structure that constantly adapts itself to new uses, new problems, and new programs. Polyvalency begins with the assumption that a perfect solution never exists. Since a problem that requires a solu-

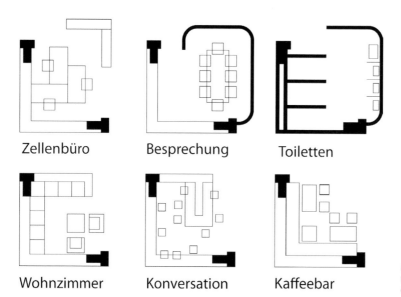

Zellenbüro	Besprechung	Toiletten
Wohnzimmer	Konversation	Kaffeebar

(4) Herman Hertzberger, various layouts of a polyvalent cell, redrawn by Andreas Rumpfhuber

tion is ever-changing and can only be temporary, Hertzberger opted for a neutral form, a form that exists through the absence of identity and distinct attributes. Therefore, the problem of adaptation is less a problem of the modification of specific attributes—as is offered by a flexible, functionalist architecture—and more a problem of the inherent quality itself.[6] Hertzberger conceived of an architecture that does not yet have an identity; thus it cannot lose identity or become chaotic if something unprecedented happens to the program.

Apart from its three-dimensionality, the significant difference is that the formerly hermetically sealed and controlled envelope of the office landscape became perforated and opened up to the city. The new headquarters for the insurance company was planned as the first element of an ample restructuring of Apeldoorn's then-periphery: the building was designed as a city within the city, and not just as a part of the city. Centraal Beheer had no designated main entrance. One could enter and leave the building at various points, according to whether you came by foot, train, bus, car, or taxi. Also breaking up the limits of the office space was a public interior street running through the building, complete with post office, travel agency, and other shops,[7] connecting the (never-realized) railway station with the

[6]   Herman Hertzberger, "The Public Realm," *A&U, Architecture and Urbanism* (April 1991), Extra Edition, E9194, p. 18.
[7]   The program of the street is as follows: newspaper kiosks, a bar, a bank, a hairdresser, an insurance agency, a travel agency, and a post office with a kindergarten, break rooms, and cafés arranged in the building and along the street; also a restaurant and, on its premises, a space for the workers' council.

city center—a kind of backbone around which all islands and thus all workplaces were oriented.[8]

The conscious use of concrete furthermore blurred the design of the polyvalent spatial structure. Is the commercial street (or the restaurant or the fitness club) inside the office building or part of public space? Contrary to the popular reading, and contrary to Hertzberger's own intentions,[9] it is not in fact the public and collective space that penetrates the office space, floating into the building and democratizing or even politicizing the workers' community: it is the other way around. By opening up the building's boundary, by diffusing and breaking up its limits, and by implementing an accessible street-like space within its confines, it is the highly controlled space of the administration that spills out into the city and impacts its different uses.

Lifelong Learning in the Factory of Leisure Time

Another example of architecture that blurs the boundaries between inside and outside—in this instance radically establishing a productive space for leisure society within its boundaries, rather than a traditional office space—is the world's first mighty space mobile, though it was never built: Fun Palace (1961–66). In their brochure, the initiators (theatermaker Joan Littlewood, architect Cedric Price, and cybernetician Gordon Pask) described the Fun Palace as a "boundless thing" and "an infinite traffic junction." As space for activity, it was to offer space for traffic. As with Centraal Beheer, Fun Palace could be reached from various points: by land, water, foot, subway, or car. It provided limitless infrastructure: without borders and with no distinct form. Fun Palace was designed as cybernetic workers' architecture for a leisure society, establishing an emancipatory program of pedagogy and collective learning within its confines. It was a subjectification machine organizing visitors' spare time according to cybernetic premises. In its programmatic conception, it expounded on the problem of a new leisure society and the expedient use of the time that is increasingly won through the soaring automation of production[10] by offering an open structure in which people could join in and learn from one another; where they could enjoy life and simultaneously emancipate themselves from a seemingly outdated labor society.

Fun Palace was a cybernetic machine for leisure time; a revolutionary apparatus that envisioned spare time as learning; an architecture

---

[8]   Herman Hertzberger, *Baudokumentatie* (Delft: University of Technology Delft, 1971), pp. 1–2.
[9]   Herman Hertzberger, *Lessons for Students in Architecture* (Rotterdam: Uitgiverij 010 Publishers, 1991), p. 48.
[10]   See Fun Palace brochure draft, Cedric Price Archive, quoted in: Stanley Mathews: *From Agit-Prop to Free Space. The Architecture of Cedric Price* (London: Black Dog Publishing, 2007), p. 70.

that prepared people for a new life outside the factory, becoming a factory in and of itself (→**5**). Fun Palace was not conceived as a passive space in which spare time just happens: its explicit goal was to usher people into a new life, activating and enlightening them. Cedric Price and Joan Littlewood's intention was that Fun Palace be a space in which people would be awakened from their apathy. It was an attempt to imagine a new life after full automation.[11] Cedric Price and his cybernetic coworker Gordon Pask intended an architecture that is never completed; a building that is never a building, without a specific form, without a specific program, and without a fixed layout; an "anti-architecture" (Price). In the words of Rem Koolhaas: "Price wanted to deflate architecture to the point where it became indistinguishable from the ordinary . . ."[12]

As architecture, Fun Palace was the representation of its cybernetic conception. Confined activity zones of various sizes—conceptually akin to Hertzberger's islands, or to the team area in the Bürolandschaft—organized the building. According to Mark Wigley,[13] the vast open scaffold was the most elaborate version of a networked incubator for leisure time associated with participatory democracy, individual creativity, and self-actualization. To Wigley, the load-bearing structure had almost disappeared, with the building only existing due to zones of activity and zones of distinct atmospheric intensity. Fun Palace was to be a building that avoids being a building: "[A] new network architecture emerges, a delicate ghostlike trace that operates more as landscape than building."[14]

Fun Palace, and in this respect also Centraal Beheer and Buch und Ton, represent architecture whose formative concept is the cybernetic network, similar to Mario Tronti's factory of society and the concept of immaterial labor. This is a network that aims to extend itself infinitely; that represents a holistic, complete world, including humans and machines on the same hierarchical level, quasi addressing them on equal terms, enabling smooth communication between all entities by establishing the same standards everywhere. It is a network architecture as infrastructure that operates in the background, transcending the old dichotomy of culture and nature and that quickly became naturalized in the years of the nineteen-sixties.

[11]   Ibid.
[12]   Rem Koolhaas, "Introduction," in *RE:CP*, ed. Hans Ulrich Obrist (Basel et al.: Birkhäuser, 2003), pp. 6–9.
[13]   Mark Wigley, "The Architectural Brain," in *Network Practices: New Strategies in Architecture and Design*, eds. Anthony Burke and Therese Tierney (New York: Princeton Architectural Press, 2007), pp. 30–53.
[14]   Ibid.

(5) Gordon Pask, Cybernetic Programming of Fun Palace, 1965
© CCA Montreal

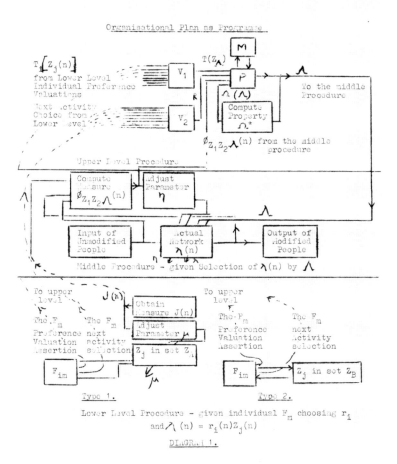

DIAGRAM 1.

Performing the Minimal Environment (on Austrian Television)

Such network architecture conceives of its users and inhabitants as mobile, nomadic subjects who are flexibly and actively appropriating space for their own uses. This cybernetic subject—the cyborg—is connected to automata and machines, passing through, inhabiting, and furnishing transitory, cybernetically organized, "non-places."[15] One outstanding architectonic example manifesting the performativity of this new subject and its new way of living was the television performance *Mobile Office* by Austrian architect Hans Hollein, aired in December 1969. Hollein delineated an exemplary nomadic,

[15]   Marc Augé, *Non-Places: An Introduction to Supermodernity* (London et al.: Verso, 2008).

(6) Hans Hollein, *Mobile Office*, performance at the Flugfeld Aspern near Vienna, Summer 1969, documentary photography © Generali Foundation, Vienna

cosmopolitan, creative workers' future and its architecture. Part of a thirty-minute TV portrait of the thirty-four-year-old architect is the 2:12-minute performance in which Hollein relates significant and typical conditions of a nomadic, immaterial, living-and-working formation to architecture and its specific quality and materiality (→**6**).

The performance starts with Hollein arriving at an airport in a small plane. He exits the plane and carries a medium-sized suitcase to the adjacent grassland. With the help of his companion, he opens the case and unfolds a translucent plastic sheet; he then connects it to a compressor, inflating the bubble. Hollein crawls into the pneumatic bubble, or *pneu*, and immediately starts to work with his legs crossed and a wooden drawing board on his knees. He draws a conventional pitch-roofed house when suddenly the telephone on his drawing board rings. Hollein talks to a client, assuring him or her that the design has just been completed, that it will be sent to her immediately and that, yes, it is a very modern design . . .

The pneumatic bubble is an architectonic prototype of a new paradigm for a creative, entrepreneurial subject: the soft and cuddly sphere isolates the architect from his or her immediate surroundings, producing an insular indoor climate in which the architect is immersed and thus—no matter where—becomes active, able to work. In other words, the bubble is—as design—the precondition for nomadic working, modulating itself from place to place. The iconic design affects in a double way. On the one hand, the bubble is its own metaphor, its own thought bubble representing the absolute monadic enclosure of the working subject attached to machines. On the other hand, the bubble is not functionally determined; it is not a production space for a group of people but, decidedly, an ironically oversubscribed, proto-typic, single workplace of a boundless daily grind.

The vast plane on which the bubble is staged is already constructed as environment and implies all the infrastructure needed for a modern life. The field is an open, extensive plane that is not yet functionally determined; it neither follows a visible grid, nor has a quantitative, observable order. The infrastructure and its knots are just there: they are assumed, requiring neither highlighting nor definition. The bubble is the extreme version of an enclosed minimal environment against the vastness. It is a kind of architecture that is an apparatus, both allowing isolation from inhospitable (man-made) ambiances—as do the space suit and the space capsule, to which Hollein so often has referred—while also allowing communication with others via cyber-netic apparatuses. Furthermore, it is an architecture that adapts itself to every single place. As an envelope conceived for an individual, the pneumatic construction actualizes itself in each and every situation and with each new program. It is, in a twofold way, programmatically open. Firstly, in its relationality toward the outside; secondly, in the way that it is, inherently, a functionally open interior. Depending on its use, the *pneu* becomes a nomadic dwelling or a workplace.

The Factory of Society and Its Architecture

The projects I have discussed all exemplify a transitory moment in which the paradigm of disclosure opens up to become the distributed workplace and Mario Tronti's factory of society. Architecture becomes standardized global infrastructure that implicitly structures the way we live and work. Former interior spaces spill out and expand into public space, merging into a typology that no longer has any outside. The economically calculated, generic and neutral space allows for constant reorganization of its use: whether undergoing temporary formations in response to an agency or housing manifold functional programs at different times. This architecture is not yet fixed in its function, meaning, or use, providing space that is first and foremost neutral. Only through its use does its organized nature temporarily solidify. This kind of configurability of space allows for the synthesis of different functions in a spatial continuum and, in doing so, keeps the space in a constant process of transformation and negotiation. It is a horizontal space in which digital machines and automats are arranged on equal terms with human beings. The laborers, the employer, and even the architects all become performative entrepreneurs, and the architects' practice tends toward that of an organizer.

Simultaneously to Buch und Ton, Central Beheer, Fun Palace, and Mo-bile Office, another paradigmatic project was being conceived. This was the much-cited No-Stop City, a project of global scale conceived

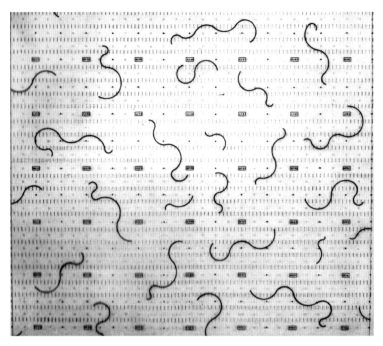

(7) Archizoom Associati, Conceptual drawing of No-Stop City, 1969

by the Italian architects' group Archizoom Associati (→**7**). From 1969, the young Italian architects and designers produced a series of drawings and collages of an infinite space that would gain rhythm only through infrastructural elements and whose different functions would be homogenously integrated into the network. Without contradiction, both production and consumption followed the same logic and the same ideology of coding. The factory and the supermarket became exemplary models of the future city: they were imagined as the potentially boundless and holistic urban structure. As Pier Vittorio Aureli has argued,[16] No-Stop City was the direct realization of Mario Tronti's idea of the factory of society. To Archizoom Associati, the city stopped being a place. The metropolis became a condition for the circulation of consumer products; the city converged with an all-encompassing capitalist market as Archizoom themselves argued: "In fact, no reality exists any longer outside the system itself: . . . The city no longer 'represents' the system, but becomes the system itself, programmed and isotropic, and within it the various functions are contained homogenously, without contradictions. Production and Consumption possess one and the same ideology, which is that of Programming."[17]

[16]   Pier Vittorio Aureli, *The Project of Autonomy: Politics and Architecture within and against Capitalism* (New York: Princeton Architectural Press, 2008).

[17]   Archizoom, "NO-STOP CITY, Residental Parking, Climatic Universal System," in *Exit Utopia: Architectural Provocations 1956–76*, eds. Martin van Schaik and Otakar Mácel (München et al.: Prestel, 2005), pp. 154–73.

The description of No-Stop City is reminiscent of an idealized model of office landscape that, ten years before, had already incorporated all of its outside areas conceptually. Its interior would not be a representation but would actually consist of information flow. Analogous to this, the urban space in the drawings of No-Stop City became a coded isotropic and worldwide system that no longer had any representational function. Thus, in principle, the contemporary city in the nineteen-sixties existed only through infrastructure. The city was dealt with as if it were an interior space: a kind of extended office landscape where furniture is arranged according to whatever situations occur. The economic planning that actually organizes the whole society to become productive eliminates the former conflict between the public and the private. In conclusion: in such a frictionless space, people can become self-empowered. They can extend the responsibility that they have gained through the new cybernetic work organization to a spectrum of other domains: housing, leisure time, governance of society. In doing so, they free us all from bourgeois society.

Conclusion

It would be naïve to see these examples of an architecture of immaterial labor—the vast planes of No-Stop City or the open scaffold of Fun Palace; Centraal Beheer's polyvalent megastructure or the flat, non-hierarchical interior of the office landscape; and Hollein's pneumatic bubble—as truly neutral and facilitative of any imaginable function and form. The possibility of these spaces is densely connected with their architectural framing, their infrastructure: with the technical and organizational underlying formation organizing the background. Ultimately, the spontaneous self-organization, self-administration, and self-exploitation of society is an illusion, and this is particularly true for the societies whose organization and functioning are highly technicized (and whose architecture is accordingly conceived in terms of infrastructure). Organization, administration, and exploitation are necessarily conditioned through the projects' infrastructural framing, their spatial organization. In this sense, architecture establishes intervals and rhythms in a territory: it constructs the framing of possibilities.

Tahl Kaminer

IN THE SEARCH OF EFFICACY
Debate and Experimentation after May '68

In the nineteen-seventies, architecture embarked on a process of re-treat from its earlier ambitions to directly affect society. This retreat was generated by several factors, one of which was the pessimistic conclusion reached by many architects and architectural critics, name-ly, that architecture is subservient to society, to politics, and to domi-nant ideology and is unable to realize projects that diverge from the contemporary status quo. The emergence of architectural autonomy as a safe haven for architecture in the discourse of the Tendenza and of Peter Eisenman was therefore very different from "the autonomy of the political" identified a little earlier by figures such as Mario Tronti and the Workerist movement in Italy: for Tronti and his allies, the au-tonomy of the political was embodied in the empowerment of politics in the Keynesian era of strong centralized governments—an era in which economics was subordinated to society and politics.[1] In archi-

[1]   See Peter Eisenman, "Autonomy and the Avant-Garde," in *Autonomy and Ideology: Positioning an Avant-Garde in America*, ed. Somol, R. (New York: Monacelli Press, 1997), pp. 68–79; Peter Eisenman, "Mis-readings", *Houses of Cards* (New York: Oxford University Press, 1987), pp. 168–86; Aldo Rossi, *The Architecture of the City* [1966], trans. D. Ghirardo and J. Ockman (Cambridge, Mass.; London: MIT Press, 1991); Massimo Scolari, "The New Architecture and the Avant-Garde" [1973], in *Architecture Theory since 1968*, ed. K.M. Hays (Cambridge, Mass.; London: MIT Press, 2000), pp. 126–45; Pier Vittorio Aureli, *The Project of Autonomy: Politics and Architecture within and against Capi-talism* (New York: Princeton Architectural Press, 2008), p. 32; Mario Tronti, "The Strategy of Refusal", in *Autonomia: Post-Political Politics*, eds. Sylvere Lotringer and Christian Marazzi (New York; Los Angeles: Semiotext(e), 2007), pp. 28–35.

tecture, the idea of autonomy increasingly dictated the interest of the discipline in its own products, processes, and methodologies, often in the complete absence of a social, economic, or political context.[2] Curiously, the perception of architecture as completely determined by society took hold precisely in a period in which many scholars abandoned monodirectional ideas about the shaping of society. Louis Althusser argued that ideological state apparatuses, belonging to society's superstructure, took an active part in shaping society[3]; Michel Foucault described how power infiltrates all aspects of society[4]; many neo-Marxists focused on issues of consciousness and culture as determining factors that supplemented society's infrastructure.[5] Consequently, while the understanding of the diverse factors and forces that shape society was widening, in architectural circles it was narrowing.

The perception of architecture as a practice subjugated by society was not limited to advocates of neoliberalism who wished to confine practices to professional know-how. The Marxist architectural historian Manfredo Tafuri wrote, paraphrasing Engels, that "just as it is not possible to found a Political Economy based on class, so one cannot 'anticipate' a class architecture (an architecture for 'a liberated society'); what is possible is the introduction of class criticism into architecture. Nothing beyond this, from a strict—but sectarian and partial—Marxist point of view."[6] Charles Jencks, in turn, argued that architecture is necessarily subservient to society, that modernism was never "progressive" as some had believed.[7]

Manfredo Tafuri was greatly influenced by the work of his peers, the philosopher Massimo Cacciari and the political scientist Mario Tronti. It can be argued that a certain perception of society, which can be identified in Tafuri's work, was borrowed from Cacciari and Tronti. The theory in question identified the manner in which a specific model of organization of production, such as the assembly line, was reproduced in all levels of society, including the structural base and the superstructure, the city and architecture. In such a worldview, the

[2]   See Tahl Kaminer, *Architecture, Crisis and Resuscitation* (London and New York: Routledge, 2011), pp. 87–113.
[3]   Louis Althusser, "Ideology and Ideological State Apparatuses," *Lenin and Philosophy and Other Essays*, trans. Ben Brewster (1970; repr., New York: Monthly Review Press, 2001), pp. 85–126.
[4]   See, among others, Michel Foucault, *Discipline and Punish* (London: Allen Lane, 1979); Michel Foucault, *Power/Knowledge*, ed. Colin Gordon (Brighton: Harvester, 1980); Barry Hindess, *Discourses of Power: From Hobbes to Foucault* (1996; repr., Oxford: Blackwell, 2001), pp. 96–136.
[5]   See, for example, Cary Nelson and Lawrence Grossberg, eds., *Marxism and the Interpretation of Culture* (Urbana and Chicago: University of Illinois Press, 1988).
[6]   Manfredo Tafuri, *Theories and Histories of Architecture* (New York: Harper & Row, 1980), p. xv.
[7]   Charles Jencks, *Modern Movements in Architecture* (Harmondsworth, Middlesex: Pengiun Books, 1973), pp. 29–94.

negative forces, such as irrationalism or nihilism, appear as necessary counterreactions that are part of the system and prevent real change. In other words, this is a very different theory of society than a Hegelian idea of progress, which identifies the determining role of the negative in social transformation. Tafuri's pessimistic comment—"one cannot 'anticipate' a class architecture"—has to be read as the statement of a radical or a revolutionary rather than a reformer.[8] It rejects the possibilities of a revolutionary architecture preceding a social revolution but says nothing about reformist architecture.

Charles Jencks claimed that architecture was necessarily apolitical. His evidence included the realization of similar buildings in capitalist-democracy and in communist states, as well as the absence of a clearly political stance by architects such as Mies van der Rohe or Le Corbusier.[9] The debate Jencks was involved in was problematic in a number of senses, primarily in the type of *politics* he was attempting to ascribe to or deny architecture. Contrasting the Western Bloc to the Eastern Bloc of the Cold War, Jencks was indeed contrasting two very different political systems and ideologies, while ignoring the fact that they shared a very similar political economy, based on Keynesian theories of governmental intervention and, to different extents, planned economies and planned societies. Working within a similar political economy, the architecture realized in these different political contexts was often similar. The differences that Jencks conveniently ignored emerge not so much in social housing in Western Europe versus housing in Eastern Europe, but in corporate skyscrapers in the United States and in the symbolism and monumentality of the *people's palaces* realized in several capitals of the Eastern Bloc. The corporate skyscrapers, commissioned by private corporations in conditions of a free real-estate market, are not found in territories without capitalism, and the people's palaces demonstrate the huge centralized power of the states of the Eastern Bloc, far exceeding that of Western governments. Jencks would have reached a different conclusion, therefore, had his emphasis been on political economy rather than on the superstructure—on politics and ideologies—and there is plenty of evidence of how political economy shapes the urban environment.[10]

[8]   This paper will follow Karl Korsch's understanding of the terms "reformist" and "revolutionary"; see Karl Korsch, *Marxism and Philosophy*, trans. Fred Halliday (1923; repr., New York and London: Monthly Review Press, 2008). See also Ernesto Laclau and Chantal Mouffe, *Hegemony and Socialist Strategy: Towards a Radical Democratic Politics* (1985; repr., London and New York: Verso, 2001), p. 61. See more in Tahl Kaminer, "Reformism, Critique, Radicalism," in *Critical Tools*, eds. Hilde Heynen, Jean-Louis Genard, and Tahl Kaminer (Brussels: La Lettre voleé, 2012), pp. 189–97.
[9]   Jencks, *Modern Movements in Architecture*, pp. 29–94.
[10]   See Tahl Kaminer, "City and Society: The Keynesian New Town and the Resurrection of Capitalism," in *The Planned and Unplanned City*, ed. Michel Provost (Amsterdam: SUN, 2010), pp. 38–43.

All this may undermine Jencks's focus on political systems, but it fits neatly with an idea of architecture being subservient to political economy. This paper will focus on a couple of examples demonstrating the possibilities of architecture achieving societal efficacy, while, at the same time, contributing to the *dead end* in the search for a radical architecture reached in the nineteen-seventies. The paper will conclude with the discovery of the possibility of realizing reformist architecture *in advance* of the related political economy. This conclusion will be wrought from the architecture of the twenties, via its revisionist interpretation in the seventies by Tafuri.

In Search of Efficacy

In France, the events of May '68 took place at the moment in which the old Beaux-Arts school was dismantled, replaced by several *Unités Pédagogiques*.[11] In the following years, sociologists, and particularly urban sociologists from Henri Lefebvre's sphere of influence, would be invited to different units and take part in radicalizing the students.[12] Among the young architects and students immersed in the radical ferment of the period was Bernard Tschumi, who worked at the time for Candilis, Josic & Woods; Candilis was the head of UP6, the most politically committed unit.[13] Tschumi was familiar with the work of Lefebvre, and he knew Hubert Tonka, Lefebvre's assistant and a member of the radical architecture group Utopie. One of Tschumi's first published projects was the ideas competition entry *Do-it-Yourself-City*, carried out in collaboration with his work-colleague Fernando Montés. The project marries a technological utopia with radical politics and is indebted to Cedric Price's *Potteries Thinkbelt*.[14] It includes diagrams, tables, collages, and axonometric drawings of small, mobile architectural objects, which were designated as urban interventions, functioning as local multimedia information and communication centers. The project expresses interests that can be associated with systems theory, cybernetics, or informatics. The ideas of "play" and "event" already appear at this early moment: "The inhabitant's disposable means," write the architects, "permit his choice of diverse degrees: change of his environment, select his informations [*sic*], provoke an

[11]   Martin Pawley and Bernard Tschumi, "The Beaux-Arts since '68," *Architectural Design* 9 (1970), pp. 533–66.
[12]   Jean-Louis Violeau, "Why and How 'To Do Science'? On the Often Ambiguous Relationship between Architecture and the Social Sciences in France in the Wake of May '68," *Footprint* 1 (Autumn 2007), pp. 7–22. Lefebvre himself would give lectures at UP7; see Lukasz Stanek, "Lessons from Nanterre," *Log* 13–14 (Fall 2008), p. 61.
[13]   Louis Martin, "Transpositions: On the Intellectual Origins of Tschumi's Architectural Theory," *Assemblage* 11 (April 1990), pp. 23–37.
[14]   See Joan Ockman, "Talking with Bernard Tschumi," *Log* 13–14 (Fall 2008), p. 160.

	activites	composants
1 AMI	ACTIVITES MILIEU IMMEDIAT espace domestique d'appoint complément d'appartement x cpt apt xx cpt apt xxx	TOURELLE LIVING PLATFORM PORTIQUE PORTE E.D. CAPSULE FENETRE
2 AMA	ACTIVITES MILIEU ADJACENT acts postscolaires acts vieux	DOME MACHINE A APPRENDRE EQ. DE JEU PANNEAU D'AFFICHAGE
3	EQUIPEMENT EXTRADOMESTIQUE sol et toit	BOITE DESTINATAIRE MODULES DOME
4	ISOLEMENT CINQ SENS	CAPSULE D'ISOLEMENT
5	PARKING DRIVE IN	MACHINE A APPRENDRE ECRAN DE PROJECTION HAUT PARLEUR MOBILE MACHINE DE VENTE
6	ACTIVITES GRAND NOMBRE sport religion politique	ENVELOPPE GONFLABLE LIVING PLATFORM HAUT PARLEUR MOBILE SIEGES TEMPORAIRES
7	CONFERENCES ECHANGE IDEES	MODULES DOME CONTAINER SIEGES TEMPORAIRES PLANS HORIZ. 78 CM
8	KIOSQUE point de distribution point concentration	LIVING PLATFORM E
9	ACTIVITES SPECIALISEES salle de consultation centre de perfectionnement commerces spéc. expositions	CONTAINER MODULES DOME MACHINE A APPRENDRE SIEGES TEMPORAIRES
0	ART EPHEMERE	GRUE LIVING PLATFORM E ECRAN DE PROJECTION HAUT PARLEUR MOBILE SUNLIGHTS ET SPOTS

23

	composants	constituants
1 ET	TOURELLE	ECLAIRAGE REGLABLE CONTAINER ET SUPPORT:EQUIPEMENT ELECTRONIQUE PROJECTEUR ET ECRAN COURTE DISTANCE RECTOVERSO ATELIER AJUSTABLE AVEC EQUIPEMENT DESSIN TRAVAIL RANGEMENT LIVRES BANDES DOCUMENTS EN OPTION: ACCESSOIRES FRIGIDAIRE THERMOREGULATEUR
2 LP	LIVING PLATFORM	STRUCTURE MODULAIRE MOBILE EQUIPEMENT ELECTRONIQUE PAR ELEMENTS INDEPENDANTS ECRANS D'ISOLEMENT RABATTABLES RANGEMENT LIVRES BANDES DOCUMENTS VETEMENTS ATELIER AJUSTABLE AVEC E.D.T. EN OPTION:LITS.CHARIOT CUISINE MINUTE.ACCESSOIRES
3 EP	PORTIQUE	ECLAIRAGE REGLABLE EQUIPEMENT ELECTRONIQUE PAR ELEMENTS INDEPENDANTS CHARIOT AUTOMOTEUR D'INFORMATION POUTRE-SUPPORT A HAUTEUR VARIABLE RANGEMENT LIVRES BANDES DOCUMENTS
4 LPE	LP EXTERIEURE	STRUCTURE MODULAIRE MOBILE ELEMENTS PAROIS EXTERIEURES ET PLANCHERS ECHELLE ACCES NIVEAU 2 ECRANS D'AFFICHAGE DEPLIABLES EN OPTION:EQUIPEMENT ELECTRONIQUE POUR VISUAL.
5 M	MODULE	ELEMENT DE SOL ET DE PAROI A:OPAQUE B:TRANSPARENT ELEMENT D'ESCALIER ELEMENT PORTE COULISSANTE
6 EG	ENVELOPPE GONFLABLE	ENVELOPPE GONFLABLE COMPRESSEUR AVEC VENTILATION ET THERMOREGULATION SAS ENTREE SORTIE
7 C	CONTAINER	CONTAINER MOBILE EN OPTION:TOUT EQUIPEMENT DETERMINE PAR ACTIVITE
8 CT	CAMION-TAXI	A: CAMION LEGER B:ESTAFETTE EQUIPEMENT RADIO CHARIOT ELEVATEUR
9 CI	CAPSULE D'ISOLEMENT	TETES ET ANNEAU CENTRAL INDEPENDANTS EQUIPEMENT ELECTRONIQUE AUDIOVISUEL ATELIER E.D.T. ECLAIRAGE REGLABLE ET THERMOREGULATION LIT-DIVAN
0 G	GRUE	

24

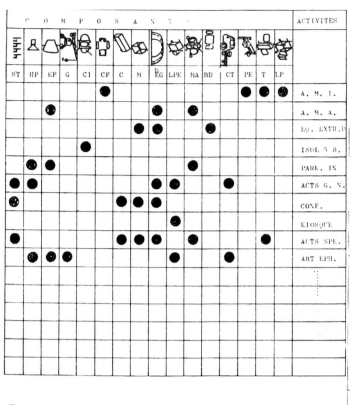

(1) Bernard Tschumi and Fernando Montés, Do-It-Yourself-City, 1969/70, Plates 23 and 24: tables listing components, constituents, and activities. Courtesy of Bernard Tschumi Architects

(2) Bernard Tschumi and Fernando Montés, Do-It-Yourself-City, 1969/70, Plate 25: allocating components to activities via architectural form. Courtesy of Bernard Tschumi Architects

event. He is able to visualize and discuss information, active reunions of persons, of artistic manifestations, as well as of games."[15]

An important section of the project is the identification of "activities" and the allocation of architectural forms to specific activities—the transition from a radical sociology to architecture (→**1**,→**2**). The activities outlined by Tschumi and Montés depart from the functionalist *needs* that dominated the previous decades. Such *needs* were embedded in a mechanical understanding of society, which reduced life to basic essentials, ignoring the communal, social, cultural, and spiritual desires of a public that had become more affluent and was no longer satisfied by pursuing the most basic means of survival. In response to the planned society, planned economy, and planned cities of the period and in reaction to the social engineering attempted by the Keynesian welfare state, certain segments of the public—most particularly the

[15]   Bernard Tschumi and Fernando Montés, "Do-It-Yourself-City,"
         L'Architecture d'aujourdhui 148 (February–March 1970), pp. 98–105.

To really appreciate architecture,
you may even need to commit
a murder.

Architecture is defined by the actions it witnesses as much as by the enclosure of its walls. Murder in the Street differs from Murder in the Cathedral in the same way as love in the street differs from the Street of Love. Radically.

(3) Bernard Tschumi, A poster from the *Advertisements for Architecture* series, 1976–77
Courtesy of Bernard Tschumi Architects

students—demanded spontaneity, freedom, and creativity. Therefore, the "activities" outlined in Do-It-Yourself-City must be understood as an attempt to infuse into the city—via architecture—the social and cultural *content* that the barren, rigid, and repetitive modernist city did not offer, including temporal and ephemeral aspects. While many of the radical architecture groups of the period were content with the creation of ephemeral inflatables as a means of inserting spontaneity, diversity, and temporality into architecture and the city, Tschumi and Montés moved a step further by developing a series of small architectural objects meant to facilitate specific activities, which, in turn, suggest self-realization in a sense that the reified and monotonous urban environment of the nineteen-sixties did not (→**4**).

The young Bernard Tschumi searched for the "environmental trigger"— a means for architectural efficacy. He concluded that knowledge of the built environment and not building "can contribute to polarising urban conflicts and inducing radical change."[16] But, in the early seventies, Tschumi discovered via poststructuralism the work of the her-

[16]   Bernard Tschumi, "The Environmental Trigger," in *A Continuing Experiment: Learning and Teaching at the Architectural Association*, ed. James Gowan (London: Architectural Press, 1975), p. 93

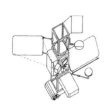

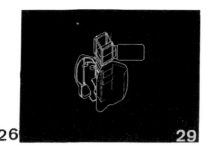

26 29 27

(4) Bernard Tschumi and
Fernando Montés, Do-It-Yourself-
City, 1969/70, Plates 26, 27 and 29:
small-scale mobile urban interven-
tions.
Courtesy of Bernard Tschumi
Architects

etic surrealist Georges Bataille.[17] The writings of Bataille offered the
Swiss architect the possibility of developing his interest in radical acts
that emphasized *transgression,* which could circumvent the need for
proof of societal efficacy. The series of posters *Advertisements for
Architecture* perfectly highlights the transition in Tschumi's thought:
the rot, excrement, and decay found in the Villa Savoye, the subject of
one of the "advertisements," comfortably fit Bataille's interest in the
obscene and excluded. However, not all traces of radical sociology are
absent in the advertisement series. The advert that depicts someone
falling—or, rather, being thrown—out of a window (→**3**) includes the
caption: "Architecture is defined by the actions it witnesses as much
as by the enclosure of its walls. Murder in the Street differs from
Murder in the Cathedral in the same way as love in the street differs
from the Street of Love. Radically."[18]
What this poster suggests is that architecture is neither the built object, nor the Cartesian space enclosed by the walls, ceiling, and floor,
but that architecture also includes the specific occurrences taking
place there. This presents an extreme expansion of the architectural
field and reflects Lefebvre's understanding of social practice as a determining factor of space. However, the roles of the building's architect and
the architectural design in initiating the event in question remain opaque.

Nanterre

The events of May '68 in Paris began not in Paris proper, but on the
new university campus in Nanterre, in the vicinity of La Défense. The
campus, designed by the architecture studio Chauliat, was a typical
example of late-modernist functionalism, with spatial segregation enhancing social segregation, functional zoning of living, working, and leisure areas, and separation of living quarters between men and women.
Lefebvre was a professor at Nanterre at the time and observed the
students' remonstrations and the manner in which they spread from

[17]   Martin, "Transpositions," pp. 26–8.
[18]   Bernard Tschumi, *The Manhattan Transcripts* (London: Academy Edi-
tions, 1994), pp. XX.

the periphery to the center, to the area of the Sorbonne. In the short book *The Explosion*, written in the immediate aftermath of May '68, Lefebvre argued that the specific conditions of the Nanterre campus had a role in generating the agitation.[19] Lefebvre identified the expulsion of the students from the city to the peripheral campus and emphasized the consequent marginalization experienced by the students of Nanterre as one of the causes of the events; not merely an expulsion to a periphery, but a periphery that included a shanty-town and a multitude of social groups experiencing similar anomie. In addition to the geographic position, the architecture—its rigidity, its totality, its standardization, and particularly the social divisions that it enhanced programmatically, spatially, and formally—was also responsible for the radicalization of students. Lefebvre describes the explosive conditions created by the placing of the different contradictions of Gaullist France in one location. The modernist architecture was created in the image of the technocracy and standardization that dominated nineteen-sixties France. It also turned the students into cogs in an assembly line via its program and organization—giving form to the Fordist project of reorganizing society as a factory, preferring efficiency and quantity to self-realization and quality of life. So the architecture exposed the ideology of society by its extremity, enabling the students to develop a consciousness of the division of labor, sexual repression, and other conditions of postwar society, which affected their daily lives.

Consequently, the students' reaction to the restriction of desire—the separation of women and men into different dormitories—was a demand for sexual liberation; the reaction to the control and limitations by university authorities was a demand for freedom in society; the reaction to the arbitrariness and opacity of power within the university was a demand for participation and transparency; and the reaction to the geographical marginalization was the creation of new centralities and subsequently the occupation of central Paris. The campus—its architecture, its layout, its program—was, therefore, a microcosm of French society under de Gaulle, and it enabled the students to scale their critique of the specific conditions on the campus to that of society at large. The students, Lefebvre wrote, "initiate a great contestation of the entire society, its institutions, its ideologies."[20]

In other words, Lefebvre identified a revolutionary role for architecture as a machine to enhance contradictions in society and generate a

---

[19]   This reading of *The Explosion* is greatly indebted to Lukasz Stanek's *Henri Lefebvre on Space: Architecture, Urban Research, and the Production of Theory* (Minneapolis: University of Minnesota Press, 2011), pp. 179–92. While Lefebvre refers to the campus and its architecture, he does not offer a rigorous critique of the architecture but rather suggests causality in a series of remarks and comments.
[20]   Henri Lefebvre, *The Explosion: Marxism and the French Upheaval* (New York: Monthly Press Review, 1969), p. 111.

popular rebellion. But, when assessing the success of the design of the campus from the perspective of its designers and authorities, it was a failure: it failed to integrate the students into society via architecture and its spatial organization. Similarly, the role of the designer of the building in Tschumi's murder poster remains irrelevant. In both cases, the action or the event appears detached from or even contrarian to the design's intentions.

While Tschumi indicted the building itself in the murder described in his poster, Lefebvre implicated the campus for generating the student unrest. Lefebvre acknowledged the symbolic role of architecture in demystifying social conditions in university and society by making apparent what is typically veiled. He further suggested that architecture not only *says* what society is, in the sense of symbolic communication, but also *does it* by exacerbating current social conditions. So architecture, according to Lefebvre, has both efficacy and political agency: it can become political by demystifying social reality via its subservience to the dominant ideology, to the political economy, and to society.

Architecture as a means of demystification—*raising awareness* and producing a consciousness of social reality—and architecture as a trigger of political agitation are certainly interests shared by Tschumi. He identifies three possible trajectories for architecture: 1) conservative—subjugated to and representing the dominant ideology and political economy; 2) critical (*commentator*)—demystifying the operation of ideology in society; 3) revolutionary—leveraging professional knowledge in order to create new urban and social structures.[21] Tschumi, expectedly, abhors the first and focuses on the latter two categories. Lefebvre, by contrast, in his attempts to discover a critical or even revolutionary role for architecture, identifies precisely such a role in Tschumi's first *conservative* category—in architecture that is subservient to the dominant ideology and political economy. Both Lefebvre and Tschumi identify the possibility of architecture assuming radical political agency, but neither can outline a prescription for the designer interested in sociopolitical efficacy; rather, the societal efficacy that can be achieved does not correspond to the designer's intentions.

The retreat in the nineteen-seventies from the search for a radical architecture is therefore explained by the *dead end* that practitioners, historians, and theorists experienced. The pneumatic balloons, ephemeral structures, spatial frames, and the expansion of the field imagined by Tschumi and others all produced little evidence of the

[21]   See Ana Miljacki, "The Logic of the Critical and the Dangers of 'Recuperation,' or, Whatever Happened to the Critical Promise of Tschumi's Advertisements for Architecture," in Heynen et al., *Critical Tools*, pp. 141–53; see also Tschumi, "The Environmental Trigger," p. 95.

designer's control of the sociopolitical effect of their designs, with attempts at radicalism ending up primarily as rhetorical statements. It is necessary, however, to counter this pessimistic conclusion with the overwhelming evidence of a tight relationship between political economy and architecture, a relationship that is never monodirectional. Also, while the search for a revolutionary architecture that would precede a revolutionary social order ended up leading to a cul-de-sac, this does not necessarily mean the same for reformist architecture.

Absent in the last decades as a result of the advances of neoliberalism, reformism suggests a pragmatic, piecemeal betterment in the lives of citizens, whether via political, economic, or other actions, in contrast to the *revolutionary,* which infers the seizure of political power via conflict and a subsequent radical transformation of society's infrastructural base. The reformists focused on issues such as universal suffrage, sanitation, housing conditions, access to health services, education, labor laws, wages, and work conditions. Reformism is thus primarily associated with the work of the social democratic parties and trade unions that accepted the principles of *bourgeois* democracy, though it is often extended to the postwar communist parties in countries such as France and Italy that were similarly integrated into the existing political process.[22] *Reformist architecture* is therefore the architecture allied to the diverse reform movements— most famously represented by the modernist architecture of postwar European social housing.

While the constitution of the welfare state can be seen as the victorious moment of reformism, galvanized by the threat of revolution, the demise of the welfare state in the last four decades accompanied the retreat from reformism in general. This represents a return of sorts to conditions that the reformist movement had succeeded in overturning during the previous era: free market, speculation, deregulation, and liberalization, as well as the decline of trade-union power, governmental intervention and control, weakened collective bargaining, and so on.

Reformist Architecture

In order to identify the potentials of realizing reformist architecture before a supportive political economy is implemented, this paper will proceed by returning to Manfredo Tafuri's argument. As mentioned earlier, the pessimism of Tafuri relates to his interest in a revolutionary architecture, but hope for reformist architecture can also be found within his work, even if this was neither his goal nor his interest. The

[22]   Reformism should not be mixed up with the pragmatism of the *third way* politics of the nineteen-nineties, which, at the end of the day, practiced a form of neoliberal economics, even if less extreme than that of a Reagan or a Thatcher.

following interpretation of the work of the architects of the Weimar Republic will be guided by Tafuri's writings—in other words, the interpretation itself is channeled through the original understanding of Weimar produced in the early seventies.

Weimar Germany was one of a number of countries in which social democratic parties took part in governments for the first time. This first experiment in social democratic government mostly fell short of the high expectations, and in this sense, Weimar's social democrats were no exception. The social democratic parties, which were still rather novel in the postwar period, were positioned in an ambiguous place between reform and revolution: on the one hand, their not-so-distant split from the communist parties meant that their ethos was still Marxist and revolutionary, that they deemed capitalism beyond reform;[23] on the other hand, they had become the political arm of the sectarian—and reformist—agenda of the trade unions, channeling the demands for higher wages and job security. The social democrats' acceptance of and participation in the *bourgeois* democratic political system necessarily meant integration, pragmatism, and retreat from revolution. To this problematic mixture, it is necessary to add the diverse political pressures felt by social democratic parties, particularly those of Weimar Germany, and the necessary compromises of coalition governments. But perhaps worst of all was the astonishingly limited economic, social, or political program of these parties in the interwar years, except for representing the interests of trade unions. The major program imagined by these parties was nationalization, but beyond a few minor and isolated cases, instances of nationalization did not take place in the social-democratic-run countries of Europe in the twenties.

The case of the Weimar social democrats was somewhat different than in France or Britain, both because of their dominance on the political stage of the nineteen-twenties and because of the Weimar Republic's association with this specific political party. The twenties were, of course, also a great decade for architectural and urban experimentation. What will be argued here, in line with Tafuri's position in *Architecture and Utopia*,[24] is that some of these experiments reproduced, in architecture and in the city, the logic of the Keynesian economy and of planism (*planisme*)—before Keynes developed his general theory or Henri de Man and the Groupe X-Crise provided an outline of planism (*planisme*). In this sense, architecture succeeded in realizing projects that were not subservient to its contemporaneous political economy.

[23]   Laclau and Mouffe, *Hegemony and Socialist Strategy*, p. 73.
[24]   Manfredo Tafuri, *Architecture and Utopia: Design and Capitalist Development*, trans. Barbara Luigia La Penta (1973; repr., Cambridge, MA, and London: MIT Press, 1976).

(5) Hans Scharoun, Villa at the Weissenhof Settlement, Stuttgart, 1927
Taking advantage of the freedom of the singular building enabled by the urban design of Mies, the villa experiments with architectural form. (Photo: T. Kaminer, 2007)

(6) Ernst May, The "zigzag houses," Bruchfeldstraße Settlement, Frankfurt-Niederrad, 1926–27 (Photo: T. Kaminer, 2007)

Two experiments of the Weimar Republic can serve here as examples of different architectural trajectories taking place in parallel: the Weissenhof housing estate by Mies van der Rohe and the "zigzag" complex at the Bruchfeldstraße estate in the Niederrad district of Frankfurt by Ernst May. The canonic Weissenhof was composed of suburban houses, *pavilions*, stand-alone, singular buildings, with a single slab by Mies *anchoring* the entire district. Built in the suburban outskirts of Stuttgart and with meandering garden-city suburb streets, Weissenhof epitomized the middle-class demand for freedom, privacy, and individuality by allowing the singular building a certain detachment and freedom from the urban whole (→**5**). In contrast, Ernst May's estate privileged the urban block rather than the singular building. The block, with its courtyard, became the *oasis* for the working class, negotiating collectivity and individuality in the urban form. The relation of the block to the city remained ambiguous: on the one hand, it was not detached from its environment via front gardens or by being raised on columns, yet, by rotating the block elements, its zigzagging façade deformed the typical street (→**6**). Each element in the block was subordinated to the logic of the whole (→**7**), whereas Weissenhof allowed significantly more freedom to the single building. However, none of these ideas were followed to their conclusion; May's block retained certain independence from the city whereas Weissenhof offered, despite the autonomy of its singular buildings, a limited *wholeness*.

The *Pavillonsystem* found at Weissenhof was identified by the architecture historian Emil Kaufmann as a reflection of the revolutionary spirit of the late eighteenth century, expressing the position of the individual in the emerging middle-class society by allowing the singular building its own autonomy, just like the elevated place of the human subject in Kant's autonomy of the human will.[25] Whereas Kaufmann sketched an associative relation, Tafuri outlined a tighter relationship by inferring that the emergence of the Pavillonsystem was related to the fragmentation and alienation of society caused by market capitalism, to the breakdown of a totality into alienated fragments, visible in the built environment as much as in society.[26] In any case, the formation of the Pavillonsystem coincided with the rise of the bourgeoisie; it emerged as the small-scale imitation of the residences of nobility by the aspiring members of the bourgeoisie; and it reflected the importance of individualism in middle-class society. Moreover, free-market capitalism in the urban environment, particularly when practiced by small- to medium-scale developers, benefited from such a system by allowing developers more freedom from the dictates of any *civic*, *bureaucratic*, or even *divine* understanding of the city as a totality—in other words, when given free rein, small-scale developers tend to create autonomous, singular buildings.

Consequently, Mies's Weissenhof can be seen as a product and representative of freedom, individualism, privacy, and free-market economics. It therefore demonstrates the manner in which architecture is determined by society, by the current political economy, and also by worldview and values. In contrast, May's Frankfurt housing estates

[25]   Georges Teyssot, "Neoclassic and 'Autonomous' Architecture: The Formalism of Emil Kaufmann," *Architectural Design 51*, nos. 6–7 (1981), pp. 24–9; Anthony Vidler, *Histories of the Immediate Present: Inventing Architectural Modernism* (Cambridge, MA, and London: MIT Press, 2008), p. 21–40.

[26]   This comment is interpretative. See, among other instances, Piranesi's "prophecies" of freedom from the organic whole in Tafuri, *Architecture and Utopia*, pp. 14–6; the freedom of the architectural fragment in the iron grid, pp. 37–9; the "autonomy of formal construction", p. 73; or the singularity of the Seagram, pp. 145–9.

100m

have been identified by Tafuri with the assembly line,[27] with the organization prescribed by Keynesian economics and planism: a comprehensive approach that emphasizes totality and thus fosters wholeness. This continuum of building and city, architecture and urbanism, and architecture and society is the architectural-urban expression of the ideal of creating a rectified society by forming a new totality in which the alienation of the individual from the whole is overcome.

In the nineteen-twenties, the precise mechanisms, and particularly the economic mechanisms, which would be put in place in the two decades following the 1929 crash were still unknown. The political conditions in the twenties that were favorable to May's work, particularly in Frankfurt, included the social-democratic federal government, the significant power of the city council, and a strong coalition of politicians, planners, and architects, which enabled the realization of the ambitious project *despite* the free-market capitalism of the era.

So, architecture preceded political economy; but some qualifications are necessary. In the immediate aftermath of the First World War, discussions of Fordism and standardization were common, and their influence on the work of the early modernists is well documented.[28] Thus, the concept of the assembly line was already disseminated and its efficiency revered. Similarly, the idea of a strong, centralized,

[27]   Ibid, p. 116.
[28]   Mark Swenarton, "Introduction," *Building the New Jerusalem* (Bracknell: IHS BRE Press, 2008), pp. 2–3.

and interventionist government had been a demand of reformers in diverse European countries, including Germany, since the eighteen-eighties, and by the nineteen-twenties it had gained traction within a significant segment of society. In this sense, Keynesian economics and planism were merely the consistent and coherent articulation of these ideas in the form of a macroeconomic theory and a technocratic theory. In other words, May's estates implemented these ideas in urban planning and design before their parallel development in other fields. This is not meant to belittle May's achievements, but rather to point out some of the necessary elements that enabled the realization of his project. To list the ingredients: a powerful position; a strong coalition of like-minded politicians, planners, and architects; a favorable government; and an emerging and widely disseminated idea, though still vague and abstract, of an alternative to the current political economy and its societal organization.

Therefore, the diverse urban and architectural experiments of Weimar—of Ernst May and Fritz Schumacher rather than Mies van der Rohe or Hans Scharoun—were carried out while there was a sympathetic political condition, but before the realization of The Plan. Or, in other words, the correct form the Keynesian Plan would take in the urban environment was discovered in Weimar architecture and urbanism *before* Keynes or de Man actually formed their theories and long before their actual implementation. This implies that while *revolutionary architecture* may indeed be impossible in advance of a social and political revolution, as Tafuri argued, *reformist architecture* can precede economic, social, and political change. In contemporary conditions, after three decades that evinced the advance of neoliberalism, the collapse of radical movements, and the retreat of reformism, including the rise of a neoliberal architecture of spectacle, hyperindividualism, and speculation, the rebirth of a *reformist architecture* would provide a long-awaited alternative and a hope for the betterment of society by way of architectural practice.

2.
THE END (AND RETURN?)
OF UTOPIA AND CRITIQUE

Ana Jeinić

NEOLIBERALISM AND THE CRISIS OF THE PROJECT... IN ARCHITECTURE AND BEYOND

A Utopia without a Utopian Project

The crisis of neoliberalism has revealed another, much deeper and more concerning one: the crisis of (any) alternative project. One might go even further and say that the neoliberal era—including its current *zombie-phase*[1]—is marked by the overall crisis of the very category of the project: be it a social, political, economic, cultural, technological, urban, or architectural one. The persistence of anti-neoliberal protests is not proof against, but rather itself an indication of, the aforementioned crisis, for as a form of political engagement, protests serve primarily to discredit the current regime and less to articulate an alternative. Without a unifying horizon—the *project* of a possible alternative world accompanied by a plausible theory of transformation toward it—protests can, at best, achieve the alleviation of the contested political practices and, at worst, provoke forthright repression and means of coercion.

In order to understand (and hopefully overcome) this particular situation in which we seem to be trapped, it is necessary to take a look at its genesis. The crisis of *grand projects* started in the nineteen-sixties with rising skepticism toward the achievements of all three mutually intertwined *super projects* of the era: modernism, technoscientism,

[1]   I refer here to the description of the contemporary state of neoliberalism as elaborated in Neil Brenner, Jamie Peck, and Nik Theodore, *Civic City Cahier 4: Afterlives of Neoliberalism* (London: Bedford Press, 2011).

and socialism. Modernism—as the cultural meta project—was questioned because of its tendency toward standardization, functionalism, mass production, and the resulting loss of individuality. Technoscientism—as the technological meta project—was accused of causing global ecological crisis. Socialism (including any form of macroeconomic *plannism*)—as the political meta project—was criticized because of its alleged association with authoritarianism, repression, and the lack of the system's capacity for spontaneous regeneration. This intellectual climate reached its peak at the onset of neoliberalism—in the years preceding and following the fall of Berlin Wall. At that time, being critical of "utopian projects" became an indispensable component of the global intellectual common sense.

Neoliberal ideology has never provided a new, comprehensive political-economic project that could be understood as an alternative to the preceding ones—it rather consciously renounced such ambitions. The ideological fathers of what later was to be called neoliberalism belonged to the most vehement critics of the very idea that social systems can and should be "planned." Their free-market mantra was explicitly directed against utopianism, plannism, and regulation.[2] They denounced all attempts at constructing a "better world" as potentially disastrous and totalitarian reveries, and instead of elaborating the theoretical foundations of an *alternative* social system, they merely proposed a set of reforms which would supposedly make the *existing* system more "efficient" and capable of spontaneous self-regulation.[3]

For sure, the critics of neoliberal ideology have rightly pointed out that neoliberalism itself is a utopia in the sense that its idealized vision of the free market (which would supposedly foster endless growth and democratization) is highly unrealistic.[4] This might sound at odds with the aforementioned anti-utopian bias of the neoliberal ideology. In order to clarify this seeming contradiction, we need to take a closer look at the very concept of utopianism that has been attributed to neoliberalism by its opponents. In the critical interpretations describing neoliberalism as a utopia in its own right, the meaning of the term

[2]   A version of anti-utopian, "anti-regulatory," and pragmatist attitude was adopted by all initial proponents of the neoliberal economic doctrine. See in particular Ludwig von Mises, *Human Action: A Treatise on Economics* (1949; repr., Auburn: Ludwig von Mises Institute, 1998) and Friedrich von Hayek, *The Road to Serfdom* (1944; repr., Chicago: University of Chicago Press, 1994).

[3]   On neoliberalism as a prolonged state of de-regulative transition (rather than a stable phase of capitalist development), see also Brenner, Peck, and Theodore, *Afterlives of Neoliberalism*.

[4]   Criticism of the utopian aspect of the economic reasoning behind contemporary forms of governance was already formulated by Foucault in his reflections on *governmentality*. See Michel Foucault, *The Birth of Biopolitics: Lectures at the Collège de France, 1978–1979* (New York: Palgrave Macmillan, 2008).

utopia is extended so as to include what David Harvey has called *uto-pianism of process*.[5] This particular form of utopianism differs from the classic utopias in that it does not provide an elaborated model of a possible, future sociospatial *formation* (social order). Instead, it provides an idealized picture of a (supposedly self-sustainable) sociopolitical *process*, without precisely defining where exactly this process should lead. Accordingly, the principle catchwords of the neoliberal ideology all express transitional processes, rather than graspable values and qualities; economic growth, democratization, deregulation, modernization, optimization, flexibility, and sustainability are cases in point. Capitalism in general and neoliberalism in particular can thus be considered utopias without a utopian project: idealized descriptions of a process, the horizon of which remains vastly undefined.

These considerations bring us back to our starting point: to the all-embracing crisis of the very category of the project, which characterizes the neoliberal era. The persistence of neoliberal policies even after the systematic discrediting of their ideological basis is a symptom of this alarming situation. The endlessly repeated excuse that serves to justify policies with undeniably disastrous effects on social and environmental well-being is grounded on a simple argument: neoliberal reforms, no matter how painful their implementation might be, are necessary, because there is no alternative to curing the "illnesses" and "degeneracies" that the failed grand projects have left in our social systems. This justification strategy could easily intimidate any alternative project in an intellectual climate where *the project as such* has become an ill-famed concept suspected of containing the germs of unfeasibility, totalitarianism, and catastrophe.

If hostility toward the project (understood as comprehensive model of a possible future) is seen as one of the basic features of neoliberalism, then approaching the *question of the project* becomes an intrinsic, primarily task of any politics aimed at overcoming the neoliberal status quo. The first step in accomplishing this task would be to reconceptualize the existing anti-neoliberal political strategies in a new manner—departing from the concept of the project incorporated in them. It is here that architecture comes into play—in a quite unusual way, considering that the relationship between architectural design and neoliberalism has hitherto been understood and studied mainly in terms of the effects that neoliberal policies have on the production of built environment.

[5]   See David Harvey, *Spaces of Hope* (Edinburgh: Edinburgh University Press, 2000), pp. 173–9.

Architecture has commonly been understood as *the* discipline of the project (*Entwurf*).[6] Different from the notion of the project in other engineering disciplines, the traditional architectural project can be considered a project in the most sublimated and socially relevant sense of the term: it is a model of a possible future situation determined by a spatial form containing and embodying a micro-level social structure. This brings us to the following point: if architecture is the discipline based on the project, and the neoliberal era is characterized by the general crisis of the latter (affecting, of course, architecture as well), then couldn't contemporary architectural practice be taken as a micro-model for exploring tactics and strategies of dealing with (and possibly overcoming) this crisis? This challenging task lies at the core of the broader research project I am currently engaged with. The text at hand is an attempt to define a basic conceptual grid, within which a parallel analysis of architectural and political strategies for dealing with the contemporary crisis of the project could be placed. At its most general level, the grid suggests dividing these strategies in two basic categories: the ones trying to reaffirm the project in this or another way, and the ones contributing to the ongoing dissolution of the project (as we knew it) and to its successive substitution by the predominantly temporal categories like process, practice, and scenario. In the following examination of these two basic tendencies, I shall try to expose their potentials and dead ends in the historical context shaped by neoliberalism and its crisis. Owing to both space constraints and the phase of my engagement with the subject, this article will *not* contain considerations on a possible solution to the problem: its ultimate scope is to provide initial analytical anchors from which the projective search for alternative solutions (alternative conceptualizations of the idea of both the architectural and the political project) could start.

In Defense of (the Utopian) Project

David Harvey has considered all traditional utopian projects (not only architectural!) as *utopias of spatial form*.[7] This is because they are always bound to a specific imaginary place and have a stable and static

[6]   The German term *Entwurf* is particularly well suited for describing this basic category of architectural practice, since its meaning lies somewhere between the English *project* and *design*. In the context of my argument, *project* is too wide of a concept, since it can refer to any personal or collective ambition, whereas *design* is too narrow, since it delimits the project of form/shape to its material/visual dimension, marginalizing its social content. *Entwurf* refers to an elaborated vision of a future situation, which can include both formal/material but also social, political, technological, and other aspects (as, for example, *Vertragsentwurf, Gebäudeentwurf, Gesellschaftsentwurf,* and *Weltentwurf*).

[7]   See Harvey, *Spaces of Hope*, pp. 159–63.

social order, which is determined and maintained by a particular spatial form. Viewed from this perspective, there is a remarkable analogy between utopias and architectural projects (as long as both are understood as projective conceptions of sociospatial form). Of course, this does not mean that all utopias are equally "architectural" or that every architectural design is utopian indeed. Utopias (of spatial form) represent rather the ultimate radicalization of the architectural project. If the rise and persistence of neoliberalism are seen as a result and expression of the general crisis of (utopian) projects, then it appears logical that the first and most obvious effect of this situation on architectural practice was the gradual decline of the utopian character of architectural design and the reorientation of the discipline toward "concrete" and "realistic" tasks.[8] Also accompanying the crisis of utopianism was the general reduction of social and political aspirations in architectural projects. Of course, this tendency did not go unnoticed by critically minded theorists and practitioners. Various strategies have been undertaken with the aim of restoring and/or rethinking the architectural project (as a project of spatial form!) on a more radical basis. To be sure, not all of these strategies promote the recuperation of the significance of architectural design by the way of its *re-utopianization*. Some of them are substantially conservative,[9] while others could most adequately be termed *analytical*.[10] However, since the main aim of this article is to examine the *projective* (that is, future-directed) dimension of architectural and political projects, I shall delimit the following analysis to those strategies that strive to defend ar-

[8]   See Tahl Kaminer, *Architecture, Crisis and Resuscitation: The Reproduction of Post-Fordism in Late-Twentieth-Century Architecture* (London: Routledge, 2011), pp. 115–67.

[9]   The response of the "conservative" strategies to the ongoing marginalization of architectural and urban design and the associated disintegration of architectural form (at the scale of the city) consists of attempts to preserve the compact forms of traditional cityscapes. Within these strategies, spatial form may be understood in two ways. It can be viewed as a consciously constructed framework within which also the idealized, traditional social form of the integrated community can supposedly be preserved (e.g., New Urbansim). Or, alternately, it can be viewed as detached from any kind of social and political meaning whatsoever, and thus laid open for serving as an instrument of neoliberal urban processes (like gentrification), beyond or against the good attentions of the involved architects (e.g., the depoliticized efforts to engender density and preserve *urbanity* typical of the European context).

[10]   Characteristic of this strategy is the position of Pier Vittorio Aureli. In his work, architectural form is deployed not as a means for preserving the traditional social or visual order, but as an instrument for framing, visualizing, and outdoing the contemporary economic and political tendencies. By this radical operation of lending form to the latent forces of the given reality, a decisive rupture is introduced into the incessant flux of neoliberal adjustment policies. For Aureli's understanding of the critical potential of the architectural project, see, for example, Pier Vittorio Aureli, *The Possibility of an Absolute Architecture* (Cambridge, MA: MIT Press, 2011) or Pier Vittorio Aureli and Martino Tattara, "Architecture as Framework: The Project of the City and the Crisis of Neoliberalism," *New Geographies* 01 (2009), pp. 39–51.

chitectural design against its ongoing marginalization by restoring its utopian aspect. The idea is that exploring the reemergence and status of architectural utopianism in the present could help us to reveal some general aspects and problems of the utopianism of spatial form as a political strategy within and against neoliberalism.

Although the rise of the neoliberal political pragmatism affected architecture in the first place by vacating the utopian content of architectural design, a particular type of utopian project—more precisely, a particular utopian motif—has started to flourish, thus becoming the universal refuge for utopian aspirations of architecture in the late twentieth and early twenty-first centuries. If we don't count the self-proclaimed utopianism of the formal experimentation characterizing the *starchitecture* of the nineties, the common denominator of the remnant grand-scale architectural utopias in the last three decades has had a concise name: *sustainable city*. It appears as if all hopes, beliefs, and ambitions of classical utopias had survived within this limited field of utopian imagination: faith in technological development (sustainable modernization); vast spatial scale of proposed interventions (master plans for whole new cities and regions); radical changes of the existing demographic structures, prevailing lifestyles, and their material conditions (geoengineering, terraforming); and the belief in definite formulas that would guarantee a good design ("form follows energy"[11]).[12]

A comparison with the architectural utopias of the past century immediately reveals an interesting aspect of the form-based architectural utopianism of our time. The prevailing types of architectural utopias in the twentieth century were either aimed at envisioning the appropriate architecture for an alternative social system (from Russian Constructivism to Constant's *New Babylon*), or at channeling the technological potentials of the existing system toward the betterment of the living standard and cultural fulfillment of the masses (from Frank Lloyd Wright and Le Corbusier to Buckminster Fuller). In contrast, the *green utopias* of the early twenty-first century are, in the first place,

[11]   Indicative of the ubiquity of this formula in contemporary architectural discourse is the number of the results found in a Google search for this phrase (more than 10,000).
[12]   These are some of the exemplary projects in this context: Foster and Partner's Masterplan for Masdar in Abu Dhabi (a newly planned, *zero-carbon, zero-waste, car-free city*), Vincent Callebaut's Lilypad (auto-suficient amphibious city for ecological refugees), Christophe DM Barlieb's Green Desert Mine (autonomous city system in the Eastern Sahara clustered around the bases of huge thermal chimneys), OMA's ZeeKracht Project (a master plan for a renewable energy infrastructure in the North Sea), Terreform's Future North: Ecotariums in the North Pole (a project for relocation of the entire existing cities into the North Pole region due to the climate change), Manuel Dominguz's Nomadic City (a project for mobile cities moving on tank wheels to the places with abundant energy sources), MAD Architecture's Superstar (self-sustaining mobile China Town), and so forth.

concerned with the possibilities of surviving the potentially disastrous consequences of the given political and economic developments hallmarked by neoliberalism (without trying to undermine or significantly rechannel these developments). In other words, if for the purpose of this argument we roughly term the first described type of architectural utopias *revolutionary*, and the second one *reformist*, then we can call the remaining, new type—with a remarkable reference to the biblical context—*salvatorian*. Two questions immediately arise from this juxtaposition. Firstly, why is it that the grand-scale utopian projects ceased to be perceived as instruments for a possible way out of the dominant political trajectories and ideologies, rather having become opportunistic and uncritical means for saving what can be saved? Secondly, if neoliberalism has always been a pragmatic, process-oriented, and anti-utopian political affair, how is it then possible that it could not only tolerate but even partially incorporate in its own functioning mechanisms a certain type of a macro-utopianism of spatial form?

As for the first question, the reasons for the decline of radical macro-utopianism on the part of the oppositional political forces lie at hand: the critical arguments against utopias formulated in the second half of the twentieth century seem to have been taken more seriously by the critics of neoliberal ideology than by neoliberalism itself. In his reflection on the utopianism of spatial form, David Harvey himself has acknowledged and neatly summarized the critique of classical utopias.[13] The argument goes that the utopias of spatial form are necessarily authoritarian, because a repressive power—supported and symbolically represented by built spatial structures—must be mobilized to maintain the social order proposed by the utopian project. A further problematic point concerns the materialization of the utopian project. The utopias of spatial form are not concerned with the processes that must be mobilized in the course of their realization. As a result, these processes tend to be either utterly violent (as is the case with revolutionary processes) or simply not viable. Critically minded architects had already become aware of these problems (immanent also to the architectural utopias of modernity) even long before they were summarized by Harvey: at the very latest with the rise of the issue of participation in the American context and with the Situationist International in the European context.

The arguments of the Situationists (and other radical leftists of the sixties and seventies) directed against the state and its authoritarian and utopian plannism were partly assimilated and rechanneled by the free-market neoliberal mantra of the eighties and nineties. Considering this, it seems all the more surprising that the *high-tech green utopianism* could resist the prevailing anti-utopian climate of the era.

[13]   Harvey, *Spaces of Hope*, p. 163.

(1) Ilkka Halso, *Museum of Nature*,
2003
Source: Friedrich von Borries,
*Klimakapseln: Überlebensbedin-
gungen in der Katastrophe* (Berlin:
Suhrkamp, 2010), p. 136

However, the perplexity disappears as soon as we consider the seemingly paradoxical alliance between neoliberal market and the state. As the critics of neoliberalism have often pointed out, the free market has never actually been free (and never could be), since its implementation, maintenance, and eventual rescuing has always been reliant on authoritarian intervention on the part of the state.[14] In other words, neoliberalism has always needed authoritarian support in saving it not from its enemies but, first and foremost, from itself. Evidently, this destructive potential does not affect merely the functioning of the global market, but also the natural resources and ecological conditions. In this light, the architectural green utopianism of spatial form appears as the summit of an authoritarian management of socioecological systems needed to provide conditions for intact accumulation of capital in the era of ecological crisis.

This feature of the contemporary utopias of sustainability did not go unnoticed by the critically minded designers. German architect and theorist Friedrich von Borries has conducted impressive research on the subject, presenting it in the form of an exhibition followed by the book *Klimakapseln* (Climate Capsules) (→**1**,→**2**).[15] Although written in the style of high-tech eco-utopias, this text turns out to be a highly dystopian vision of an extremely totalitarian, exclusive, and unjust

[14]   See, for example, David Harvey, *A Brief History of Neoliberalism* (Oxford: Oxford University Press, 2005).
[15]   Friedrich von Borries, *Klimakapseln: Überlebensbedingungen in der Katastrophe* (Berlin: Suhrkamp, 2010).

(2) Haus-Rucker-Co, *Oasis Nr. 7*,
1972, Kassel, documenta 5
Source: Friedrich von Borries,
*Klimakapseln: Überlebensbedin-
gungen in der Katastrophe* (Berlin:
Suhrkamp, 2010), p. 138

society, which lives encapsulated in the protective capsules needed
for providing a habitable life after the ecological catastrophe.[16] In the
manner of Superstudio's *Twelve Cautionary Tales for Christmas*, Friedrich von Borries captures the alarming tendencies of the present and
extrapolates them into an imaginary future. Thus, even though the
form of the utopian project is used, its direction is reversed—instead
of being a project for the future, utopia becomes a critical reflection
on the present, losing in this way its *projective* character and becoming a primarily *reflexive* tool. But if the oppositional utopian project
ceases to be a *project* itself (inasmuch as the latter is understood as
a *positive* proposal for the future), what does that mean for the oppositional architectural and political practice? Is there another way of
thinking the project? Or could the alternative to the neoliberal (non-)
project itself be a *non-project*—that is, a strategy that deliberately
rejects providing a comprehensive projection of an alternative urban,
social, political, cultural, and/or technological formation? In approaching the latter question, let us have a look at the opposite way of dealing with the contemporary crisis of projective thinking.

Dissolution of Spatial Form (or the Project without a Project)

If at the one pole of contemporary architecture's responses to the
neoliberal crisis of *projectivity* we find a peculiar comeback of the
macro-utopianism of spatial form (stamped by the magic word *sus-*

[16]   For another interpretation of Borries's book *Klimakapseln* in the context
of contemporary utopianism, see Mara-Daria Cojocaru, *Die Geschichte
von der guten Stadt: Politische Philosophie zwischen urbaner Selbstver-
ständigung und Utopie* (Bielefeld: Transcript, 2012), pp. 218–37.

tainability), then the opposite pole is marked by the process-based, distributed, micro-scale design practices that include miniaturization, fluidization, and temporalization of spatial form to a larger or smaller extent. Within these strategies, the form has mostly been subordinated to the process of its creation and transformation—sometimes up to the point where it has all but dissolved. In this context, we could rightly speak of the disappearance of the architectural project (as we knew it). It would be misleading to put all design paradigms concerned with spatial practices and processes (rather than forms) under the same umbrella, since they include such different approaches, including experiments concerning the retreat of the author from the design process; parametric design; development of open-ended sociospatial scenarios; flexible strategies in urban design as a critique of top-down master planning; participatory design; ephemeral and mobile architectures, et cetera. However, it would go beyond the scope of this article to analyze each of them separately and to reflect on their specific relation to the neoliberal ideology. Since the initial point of my considerations was the question of (missing) alternatives to neoliberalism, the following analysis will be limited to those process-based design strategies that have been either deliberately developed or retroactively interpreted as critical of neoliberalism.

In his recent publication *Distributed Agency, Design's Potentiality*,[17] art historian Tom Holert has offered a short theory of architectural and artistic engagement that can be seen as a manifesto proclaiming modest, embedded, collective, and strategic design practices instead of the grand-scale, visionary, autonomous, and static projects associated with modernist utopianism.[18] The central argument of the booklet brings about a new notion of the designer as a practitioner involved in a set of distributed micro-practices. These, according to Holert, could contribute to a gradual transgression of the operational patterns of neoliberal capitalism through the ongoing work of recycling, recomposing, and recoding the given reality. Symptomatically, Holert consciously avoids describing any exemplary *projects*, because his theory proposes a deliberate anonymization and moderation of the design practice up to the point where *designer* becomes the name of an attitude, rather than of a specific profession. A similar argument has been made by Peter Mörtenböck and Helge Mooshammer. In *Netzwerk Kultur: Die Kunst der Verbindung in einer globalisierten Welt*,[19] the two authors reflect on architectural/artistic practices that

[17]   Tom Holert, *Civic City Cahier 3: Distributed Agency, Design's Potentiality* (London: Bedford Press, 2011).
[18]   For a detailed analysis of Holert's argument, see my review entitled "A Strong Argument for a Weak Theory (of Design)," *GAM* 09 (2013), pp. 212–5.
[19]   Peter Mörtenböck and Helge Mooshammer, *Netzwerk Kultur: Die Kunst der Verbindung in einer globalisierten Welt* (Bielefeld: Transcript, 2010).

(in their opinion) can induce reconfigurations and transformations of sociophysical space. However, these transformations are not attained by means of a project of spatial form but are rather achieved in the very performance of networked architectural/artistic operations. As an example, the authors refer to the project called *Lost Highway Exhibition*, to which I shall come later.

Both Holert's and Mörtenböck/Mooshammer's conceptions of architectural/artistic practice are related to the deliberately "weak" and "non-radical" contemporary theories of political agency, such as actor-network theory, queer theory, post-operaist theories, and so forth. Within this huge and highly heterogeneous "pool" of theoretical concepts, the one that stands out for its explicit process- and network-based character, as well as its accent on self-organization, is Antonio Negri and Michael Hardt's concept of the *multitude*.[20] The term *multitude* is meant to describe the democratically organized, potentially oppositional new class emerging out of contemporary global capitalism (or, as Negri and Hardt term it, the *empire*). The following three aspects of the concept are important in our context. First, it is related to a substantially *process-based* (de facto Hegelian) argument claiming that the classes exploited in capitalism have been proceeding toward increasingly democratic forms of organization. Second, the organizational form of what the two authors consider the advanced form of democracy is that of the *network*.[21] Third, and most importantly, the concept of the *multitude* dissolves and reduces the goals and programs of political struggle to the form and practice of political organizing. In other words, the democracy of the *multitude* is not a political *project*, but rather a dynamic and spontaneous phenomenon, which emerges in the very process of political contestation.

Let me now suggest a particular (and, at first glance, somewhat peculiar) context for testing the above-exposed theories of architectural and political agency: the post-Yugoslavian landscape of transitional architectures and politics. The reason for this choice lies in the particular shape of economic/political transformations characterizing the region after the breakdown of the socialist project and the subsequent violent dissolution of Yugoslavia. The destructive effects and complexity of these processes made the integration of post-Yugoslavian countries into the neoliberal flux of undisturbed capital circulation somewhat controversial and complicated. The unconditioned liberalization and invasive internationalization of markets have been paralleled in this case by the emergence of manifold informal economic networks,

---

[20]   See Michael Hardt and Antonio Negri, *Multitude: War and Democracy in the Age of Empire* (New York: Penguin Press 2004).
[21]   In this context, it is important to note that the network as a spatial figure or metaphor is thoroughly antagonistic to the concept of spatial form, since it is made up of pure relations and processes and is virtually endless and all-encompassing.

spontaneous survival strategies, and ephemeral social and spatial configurations. These include the manifold illegal marketplaces typical of the nineties, uncontrolled urban developments (mostly parasitizing on the existing infrastructure), spontaneous appropriations and adaptations of the abandoned, formerly state-owned industrial and military facilities, but also the cooperative home-to-home networks for the exchange of goods and services, and independent (often squatted and partly unofficial) spaces for artistic and media activities (→3,→4). The relationship between these "alternative" practices and the institutional politics is anything but simple: while they are not directly integrated into the official (neoliberal) economy, they cannot in any case be considered alternative economic projects, since their relationship to the formal economic processes is mostly a parasitical one. Furthermore, many of them are equally ambivalent from the ethical standpoint: although they might represent remarkable examples of creative organizational strategies, they often embody forms of exclusion, violent dispossession, and unjust distribution (sometimes even worse than those in the formalized and legalized processes of neoliberal economic exploitation).

Urban and architectural expressions of self-organized survival practices in the post-Yugoslavian context have been the subject of polarized and controversial research and interventions on the part of academic architectural culture. On the one hand, the prevailing attitude among educated architects toward the "wild architectures" of the (never-ending) transitional era has been a mixture of disregard and scornful criticism. On the other, the "progressive" stream of younger and mostly internationally acting researchers and practitioners has increasingly interpreted these architectures as fascinating expressions of inventive, non-hierarchical, and non-ideological practices, which ignore the territorial divisions imposed by nationalist ideologies and the absurd laws imposed by transitional bureaucracies. Since the late nineties, a series of architectural/artistic projects (mostly combining research based on visual mapping with small-scale interventions) has been devoted to the post-Yugoslavian informal spatial practices.[22]

One of the most extreme examples of the research and design procedures characterizing these projects is the *Lost Highway Expedition*, which took place in 2006 (and was later enthusiastically portrayed by the same Peter Mörtenböck and Helge Mooshammer[23]). The goal

[22]   Some exemplary projects in this context include: *Genetics of the Wild City*—a STEALTH Group's research on the informal urban developments in Belgrade; Azra Akšamija's study of the self-organized inter-ethnic cooperation at the Arizona Market in the Brcko District (Bosnia and Herzegovina); Srdjan Jovanovic Weiss's numerous studies on transitional *turbo-architectures*, ETH Basel's research project *Belgrade: Formal Informal*; and some of the case studies developed within the Harvard Graduate School of Design's *Project Zagreb*.
[23]   See Mörtenböck and Mooshammer, *Netzwerk Kultur*, pp. 11–7.

of the expedition, which gathered together numerous architects, artists, and thinkers, was defined as follows: "A multitude of individuals, groups and institutions will form a massive intelligent swarm that would move roughly along the unfinished *Highway of Brotherhood and Unity* in the former Yugoslavia. . . . The reason for the *Lost Highway Expedition* is to find and study missing relationships on the highway and look at them as a model for diverse Europe."[24] During the exhibition, which lasted for about a month, the participants were pursuing their individual (though sometimes interrelated) architectural, artistic, and research practices; they were exchanging their ideas in the form of discussions, workshops, performances, and presentations—both within the group and with local supporters and audiences in the cities located along the exhibition route. Networking—in a sense of creating new productive associations in order to reconnect and re-map the fragmented territory of the former state—was understood not only as a possible positive side effect of the project, but as its primary content. One of the essential qualities of the operation—seen from the perspective of Mörtenböck and Mooshammer—is that the emergent network of relationships remained flexible and endlessly open: the project did not determine (either through fixed institutional arrangements or through materialized spatial forms) what and who could be included and what and who would have to be excluded from the network. In other words, *Lost Highway Expedition* deliberately eschewed filling the ideological vacuum left after the breakdown of the communist ideology with any fixed and clear alternative content. Thus, by carefully avoiding anything that could be considered a definite, universalist, ideological, and authoritarian proposal, it renounced its status as *project*—at least in the traditional sense of the term.

However, let us now forget for a while the optimistic perspective of Mörtenböck and Mooshammer and instead ask ourselves what critical potential projects like *Lost Highway Expedition* really have (or do not have) in the face of rising economic injustice, impoverishment, and indebtedness in the ideologically and materially deserted spaces caught in the web of neoliberal globalization. This potential remains deliberately reduced to finding and establishing alternative sociospa-

(3) Improvised and/or illegal infrastructure and houses around Arizona Market in Bosnia and Herzegovina, documented by Azra Akšamija, 2001
Source: Azra Akšamija, *Arizona Road*, Master's Thesis (Graz: Graz University of Technology, 2001), p. 34

[24]   See the official presentation of the project at http://www.schoolofmissingstudies.net/sms-lhe.htm (accessed July 2013).

tial connections not (yet) established within the formal economies and official policies. However, the absence of any determined *projective content* (or of any notion of a utopia of spatial form) makes it impossible to establish a stable criterion by which the emergent networks of opposition can be distinguished from those of exploitation. If we go back to the theory of Negri and Hardt, this critical insight into the conception of architectural/artistic practice embodied by the *Lost Highway Expedition* reveals that the concept of the *multitude* cannot provide a feasible alternative to the forces of neoliberal capitalism, so long as it does not incorporate any determined and unifying *project* apart from its organizational figure (the idealized figure of the ever-evolving, non-hierarchical, transient network). In other words, so long as such project is rejected, the networks of the *multitude* will continuously merge with and get dissolved within the networks of the *empire*.

(4) Improvised and/or illegal infrastructure and houses around Arizona Market in Bosnia and Herzegovina, documented by Azra Akšamija, 2001
Source: Azra Akšamija, *Arizona Road*, Master's Thesis (Graz: Graz University of Technology, 2001), p. 35

Facing the Gordian Knot

The exposition of the dead ends of the two radical responses to the neoliberal crisis of *projectivity* confronts us with an awkward question. If grand utopian projects necessarily bear the germ of totalitarianism, and the strategies that renounce the project (resorting to micro-practices and distributed processes) are suspected of inefficiency and potential dilution, then what form might the alternative project to neoliberalism take? Trying to formulate a quick answer to this question would imply underestimating its importance and complexity. There is only the conclusion that can be reached based on the afore-exposed considerations: the idea of the project capable of overcoming the present status quo will have to outline the form of a possible better world, while simultaneously taking into account processes of transformation toward it; to determine a horizon of emancipatory change but allow for its constant redrawing; and to entail a macroscopic model but presuppose that the transition would rather be initiated by microscopic practices. In my view, a yet-to-come reconceptualization of the project capable of meeting these claims is the most challenging and indispensable task of architectural theory, if it has the ambition of fostering design practice that could rightly be considered anti-neoliberal.

Rixt Hoekstra

NEOLIBERALISM AND THE POSSIBILITY OF CRITIQUE

For the past fifty years or so, a critical attitude toward society has been the hallmark of the *progressive* architect. In architecture today, it is the very possibility of being critical that stands at the center of debate, fueled by such question as: What is the agenda on which we should base our criticism? Is there still a public tolerance toward criticism? In the world of art and architecture, *criticality* seems to have become no more than a marketing tool: a term that has long since lost its edge, its ability to be painful.[1] Critique seems to belong to an old world, where there was still a division between the political left and right; where there was an enemy to fight against and a system to oppose. Also outside of the world of architecture, the demand for a convincing critique of society fueled by a vision of a better world constitutes one of the most difficult challenges of our neoliberal age. This led the Dutch philosopher Frank Ankersmit to state that we live in a world without alternatives, that we are caught in the politics of the inevitable.[2] In Ankersmit's view, it is symptomatic that the financial crisis is discussed exclusively in terms of a possible solution and not in terms of its causes. Such a discussion would directly put forward the question as to an alternative, and thus make clear that there is no

[1]   On this theme, see, for example, Sven Lütticken, *Geheime Publiciteit: Essays over hedendaagse kunst* (Rotterdam: NAi Uitgevers, 2005).
[2]   Frank Ankersmit, "Zonder ideologische strijd over de kredietcrisis zijn bezuiningingen voldongen feiten—we berusten in de politiek van het onvermijdelijke," *NRC Handelsblad*, May 14, 2011.

longer an ideological space to formulate such an alternative. Thinking about a better world seems to have vanished into oblivion together with the political ideologies, whether from the right or from the left. Nowadays, according to Ankersmit, we are told that we have only one choice and that the light will otherwise be extinguished. So much for democracy and free choice. It appears that Herbert Marcuse was right after all, when in the nineteen-sixties he stated that bourgeois capitalism blackmails us with the choice between total disaster or the acceptance of the system.[3]

In architecture, the idealist delirium of the nineteen-sixties and seventies is over and has been exchanged for a much more pragmatic attitude. In this respect, it is telling that the role of theory is diminishing within the discipline. Buildings today are no longer erected by the logic of meaning and metaphor, as the translation of *theory* into *practice*. In the nineteen-eighties, for example, the philosophical concept of deconstructivism influenced the experimental work of architects like Coop Himmelb(l)au, Eric Owen Moss, and Daniel Libeskind. Today, in the majority of cases, architectural developments occur without a reflective philosophical context. Buildings now constitute a *performance*: they may be marked by such elements as technological innovation and environmental achievement, but they are no longer inspired by theory. Buildings today may look spectacular, but they no longer carry any reflexive, let alone critical, charge.

Architecture thus seems to be shifting away from a long-held tradition in which experimental avant-garde buildings were always also an intellectual provocation.[4] At the same time, *criticism* and *criticality* are buzzwords that appear in many texts on art and architecture. They are as widely used as they are undefined.[5] Are they to be regarded as sad souvenirs from a world that has long since passed by? The uncertainty about architecture's critical function seems to mark the most recent age in architecture.

At the same time, as I will highlight in this article, the current debate is also a phase in a longer development that extends over a century. Moreover, as already indicated above, the discussion about critique not only takes place in architectural circles but rather concerns society at large. During the entire twentieth century, discontent and uncertainty about the role of critique led to dispute and debate. However, as I will argue here, there was a moment when the debate about critique became particularly intense. This was when different attempts

---

[3]   Ibid.
[4]   Scott Johnson, "Once Theory to Practice, Now Practice to Theory?"
        Harvard Design Magazine 33 (Fall–Winter 2010–11), pp. 5–10.
[5]   Sven Lütticken, writes: "There are more critics than ever before, but
        the Tate Gallery and the Gagosian—and most glossy art magazines—
        are just as poorly interested in art as a critical project as Time Warner
        or *Time*." Lütticken, *Geheime Publiciteit*, p. 5. Translation by the author.

were made to overcome the reductivism and perhaps also naiveté of the conventional, *oppositional* notion of critique.

However, before we dive into this history, it is important to linger for a moment on the meaning of the word *critique*. The term critique comes from the Greek verb *krino*, which means to distinguish, to discriminate. So *critique* implies being able to see differences and judge those differences and subjecting their poles to value judgments: are they good or bad, beautiful or ugly, just or unjust? Seen from this perspective, the word "critique" poses one fundamental question: What is good and what is bad in what I see around me?[6]

The wrong and the right side of cultural expression were still very clear to Max Horkheimer and Theodor W. Adorno when, in 1944, they wrote the book *Dialectic of Enlightenment*.[7] In 1944, driven by the tragic ways of history, Horkheimer and Adorno had lost what had always been the motor of their intellectual energy: the belief that the Enlightenment would contribute to the betterment of human life. Following dialectical argumentation, Horkheimer and Adorno became convinced that the Enlightenment had turned its powers against itself. Instead of leading to emancipation, reason had subjected man to an instrumental and cruel calculus. The critique they consequently developed was of *oppositional* nature: by distinguishing—in the Greek sense—a good and a bad guy, they were taking a stand against the modern world. Thus, in the most influential essay of the book called "The Culture Industry," they protested against what they saw as the growing standardization and industrialization of culture. In our modern mass culture, they said, everything is reduced to a "package": it is offered as a calculated, tailor-made unity in which all is said and done for the consumer. Culture, they stated, had become an industry, suited for the world of capitalism—and for the lazy consumer. This was oppositional critique in the true sense of the word: attacking the system and its perverse outcomes. However, while criticizing modernism in this way, they also created a problem for themselves. It was exactly in the field of music, the specialist area of Adorno, that their oppositional critique became most problematic.

In the nineteen-sixties, Adorno and Horkheimer condemned the rise of popular music. This was another *bad guy*, another product of the culture industry. However, at the same time, during that decade there was a new form of critical engagement that was expressed through pop music—think of the protest song. While Adorno saw

---

[6]   Marlies Philippa et al., eds., *Etymologisch woordenboek van het Nederlands* (Amsterdam: Amsterdam University Press, 2007), part 3, p. 133; P.A.F. Van Veen, ed., *Etymologisch woordenboek: de herkomst van onze woorden* (Utrecht: Van Dale Lexicografie, 1989), p. 421.

[7]   Max Horkheimer and Theodor Adorno, *Dialectic of Enlightenment: Philosophical Fragments*, ed. Gunzelin Schmid Noerr, trans. Edmund Jephcott (Stanford: Stanford University Press, 2002).

the importance of this phenomenon, he still condemned it. Popular music turned the suffering of the world into a form of *Warenkonsum* (consumption commodity), he said, into a form of amusement and consumption.[8] To Adorno, it was therefore the most perverse of all forms of "industrial culture." At the same time, reality proved Adorno wrong: in the sixties, when *Dialectic of Enlightenment* was finally read by a wide audience, the opposite of what he had prophesized was happening. Through new media such as television and new cultural genres like pop music, people developed a new critical conscience about their own role in society. Far from being slaves of the culture industry, people began to use their participation in culture as a point of departure for criticizing society: its outdated hierarchical character, for example, or the political abuse of scientific knowledge. As demonstrated by the Woodstock Festival—billed as "An Aquarian Exposition: 3 Days of Peace & Music"—the new popular culture did not produce a passive audience, as Adorno had predicted, but, on the contrary, a highly active one. Now where did that leave the concept of oppositional critique?

In the nineteen-sixties, it was the literary historian Stuart Hall who took up this problem.[9] In 1964, Hall broke away from the comparative literature department of Birmingham University to co-found the Centre for Contemporary Cultural Studies. Hall reacted to the commercialization of culture by starting a broad critique that would expose the relationship between culture, society, and politics. In a certain sense, it may be stated that Stuart Hall departed where Adorno and Horkheimer had left him in the sixties: if popular culture proved itself an agent of significant cultural and social change, then it had to be dignified and made into a theme of proper academic study. At the same time, Hall realized that Adorno's critical remarks about the protest song being a hit record were not entirely wrong: the forces of commercialization were unmistakably at work in popular culture. For Hall, culture was now in possession of a Janus head: it was a force of emancipation and also a form of commercialization. This duality confronted the new field of cultural studies with its most important challenge, as it had to position itself vis-à-vis popular culture and come to terms with its ambivalence. If culture was not only the perverse outcome of a corrupted system but also a multifaceted manifestation displaying both good and bad sides, then where did that leave the critic? The simplicity of the concept of oppositional critique by Adorno and Horkheimer seemed to

[8]   See the interview with Adorno on YouTube: "Adorno about Popular Music," http://www.youtube.com/watch?v=Xd7Fhaji8ow (accessed May 2012).

[9]   This paragraph is based on Tahl Kaminer, "Undermining the Critical Project: The postcritical 'third way' and the legitimating of architectural practices," *The Architectural Annual 2004–2005* (Delft: Delft University of Technology, 2005), pp. 70–3.

have disappeared. Stuart Hall declared that if culture had become an industry, then one should acknowledge the active participation of that industry in society. What Hall implicated was that culture, in other words, was not only a matter of *false consciousness* as traditional Marxist theory would have it, but an active force that constitutes society. However, this made the position of the critic far more problematic. Where oppositional critique had placed itself outside and against society, cultural critique in turn saw itself *embedded* as part of an equally embedded culture. As Richard Johnson, Stuart Hall's successor in Birmingham, claimed: "cultural studies are necessarily... implicated in relations of power. It forms a part of the very circuits it seeks to subscribe."[10] Critique could not be formulated any longer from a luxurious position outside of society, for it was already a part of it, of its discursive circuits, indeed, of the textual part of its culture industry. In the end, this was the consequence of living in an inclusive society that swallows all: culture and critique in equal measure. This of course complicated and ultimately weakened the position of the critic: from its *embedded* position, cultural criticism was not merely an observer but just as much an offender. In other words, if oppositional critique was no longer an effective and convincing instrument, then an equivalent form of societal critique was hard to find.

Meanwhile, architecture seemed to escape from the difficult position in which cultural studies found itself. In architecture, the discourse in the seventies was dominated by an attack on the utopian character of modern architecture, regarded as an authoritarian and changeless image of *liberated society*. However, this critique on the modernist enterprise was not followed by an attempt to start a new critical project, accompanying for example the rise of postmodernist architecture. Instead, fascination for reality now took the place of the fascination for utopia. This need could take different forms: for example, with a focus on subcultures, on the mundane and the popular, as in the case of Robert Venturi and Denise Scott Brown's *Learning from Las Vegas* (1972). However, this new focus on reality was more than just an innocent study project. With the examination came the affirmation of reality: with the entrance into postmodernity, the discourse became lighter, less focused on change and intervention in reality. Where the modernist architect would state, "this is how it has to be," the postmodern architect would instead assert "this is how it is." Here, too, architecture took a different route with respect to cultural studies. While studies by Rem Koolhaas, such as *Mutations* (2000) or *The Harvard Design School Guide to Shopping* (2001), resembled the agenda of cultural criticism in the seventies—demolishing cultural hierarchies

[10]   Ibid., p. 72, quoting from Robert Hewison, *Culture and Consensus: England, Art and Politics since 1940* (London: Methuen, 1995), p. 207.

so as to place shopping malls side by side with museums—at the same time there was also a crucial difference. While cultural studies had studied mass culture with an agenda in hand that was still critical, in the case of Koolhaas that balance seems to have shifted toward an acceptation and perhaps even legitimization of consumer society— the so-called "¥€$ regime."[11]

"The either/or world has become an illusion," noted Dutch architectural theorist Roemer van Toorn in 1991, and "there is no longer any sympathy with the permanent criticism of society or with the paralyzing impossibility of making a better world."[12] These words signaled the departure from critique and the entrance into the realm of so-called *postcriticism*. Criticism was now disqualified completely as a useless ensemble of opinions, metaphors, and rhetoric without any influence on reality. "Let's be useful for a change," said architectural historian Wouter Vanstiphout when he agreed to cooperate with project developers and local governments in 2005.[13] Indeed, in the Netherlands the postcritical debate coincided with the start of a new cultural practice. In these projects, the *embeddedness* of culture was taken to an extreme. As part of a new policy to revitalize run-down modernist housing estates, inhabitants were evicted and neighborhoods were demolished. Artists and architects were now called upon by those in power to offer some kind of consolation and to help reconcile the inhabitants with their destiny. So people were forced to leave their homes, but at least they had an artist painting a nice symbolic painting on the walls of their soon-to-be-destroyed apartment building.

This was the reality of the embedded *cultural practitioner* helping out in a neoliberal, profit-driven society. For the artist and the architect, the new policy also seemed like an opportunity.

Accompanying the disqualification of *useless* critique was the chance to no longer stand aside and observe, from a critical point of view, what was happening. Now was the time to really be a player among the players, to have real influence and actually play a part in what was happening in the city. However, this new relevance of artists and intellectuals came at a price.

The reaction came in the year 2007, when the research group BAVO published the book *Too Active to Act*.[14] By serving as cultural therapists of sorts, artists and architects had completely surrendered to the system, according to BAVO. Yes, these cultural actors were en-

[11]   Silke Ötsch, "Des Königs neue Firma: Inside the global ¥€$ . . . and how to get out," *GAM 04: Emerging Realities* (2007), pp. 1–13.
[12]   Roemer van Toorn, "The Society of the And (An Introduction)," *Hunch* 1 (1999), p. 90.
[13]   Quoted from http://www.strangeharvest.com (accessed April 2013). Now also printed in BAVO, *Too Active to Act: Cultureel activisme na het einde van de geschiedenis* (Amsterdam: Valiz, 2010), p. 14.
[14]   Ibid.

gaged, but their commitment was of an obedient sort, leaving behind an engagement that is maladjusted, troublesome, and, indeed, not helpful to those in power. The paradox behind their actions was that they were so keen on being helpful—on doing and acting and leaving behind all the theoretical fuss—that at the same time they did nothing. They were too active to act. Real influence and real impact, so stated BAVO, could only come from the formulation of a personal, autonomous point of view. And that was exactly what collaboration with the system had prevented artists and architects from doing. This was the consequence of their *embedded* position: surfing the winds of the ¥€$ regime, affirming the status quo, had led them away from the establishment of their own emancipatory program.[15]

At the same time, their analysis confronted BAVO with a huge challenge. They had diagnosed the disease, but what was the remedy? How could they prevent themselves from falling into the same pitfall as their opponents? BAVO came up with the concept of so-called overidentification.[16] The idea was to take over the logic of the enemy and blow it up so that it becomes grotesque, absurd, larger then life. That is, the enemy is *persiflated* until the moment his tactics are rendered useless. However, what BAVO essentially did was to stay within the system, to maintain *embeddedness*. There is still a dependency on the discourse of the opponent, only now the discourse is not affirmed but rather made absurd. Their critique is analytic of character—like a comment on the enemy, yet without being propositional in the sense of suggesting another, alternate project to that of neoliberalism.

This brings us to what I think is one of the main difficulties of the neoliberal era. As Adorno and Horkheimer noted, art and architecture have become a part of the culture industry. Since the days of Stuart Hall in Birmingham, it has become clear that culture is not only embedded in our society but is practically swallowed by it. More than ever, the problem involves figuring out how to jump out of the system, to escape from its clutches and formulate an alternative. This is what the philosopher Frank Ankersmit meant when he said that we are caught in the politics of the inevitable. It has led some thinkers to state that liberalism is of totalitarian character. At the start of the twentieth century, the social scientist Friedrich Pollock already predicted that, through its own mechanisms of control, capitalism would eventually turn into a totalitarian form of power.[17] At present, liberalism can also

---

[15]   See: ibid., p. 9.
[16]   BAVO derives the concept of overidentification from, among others, the practices of the Slovenian punk band Laibach. Under the Tito regime, they developed a new way of protesting against the regime by exaggerating its logic and by playing devil's advocate. The philosopher Slavoj Žižek is also important for BAVO in this respect. See BAVO, *Too Active to Act*, pp. 106–13.
[17]   See, among others, Friedrich Pollock, "State Capitalism," *Zeitschrift für Sozialforschung* 2 (1941), pp. 200–25.

be described as a torso with no arms or legs. The torso cannot move, cannot go forward and pursue a certain goal in this way. It is inert and static and can only endlessly circulate ideas and notions within its own belly. This seems to be the fate of our society once the great narratives of progress and social betterment have been left behind. It also means that the pretensions of a critical architecture—or, indeed, a critique of society—no longer have a *natural* place in our society, as they still did in the days of the grand narratives. Does this mean that critique is dead? That it is a pathetic anachronism of the past?

I contend that the danger of *embedded* culture and the ultimate absorption of architectural production by neoliberal politics is first of all present on the level of language. In the recent past, architectural practitioners and theorists not only accepted the neoliberal discourse but also incorporated it as their own. This is the danger of taking your partner in dialogue seriously: one is pulled into the discourse of the partner up to such a degree that one loses an own autonomous vocabulary. In other words, it seems as if contemporary architects believed in the discourse of neoliberalism up to such a point that architectural discourse lost its own autonomous identity as a consequence. No longer is there a separate vocabulary or autonomous discourse with which to counter the statements of the opponent: hence the critical deficit of architectural culture today. This is also the attraction that Adorno and Horkheimer's words have upon us now: they were *par excellence* the owners of an autonomous critical vocabulary for countering the tendencies of their times. They were authentically critical up to a degree that, to us today, seems forever lost.

The only way out of the deadlock of embedded culture, then, seems to imply leaving the paradigm of neoliberalism, breaking out of its clutches. Within that paradigm, critique may be nothing more than an anachronism. However, if we are able to free ourselves from the chains of the neoliberal ideology, a convincing social alternative to neoliberal practices may still be found. This project only has a chance once the architect is willing to let go of servitude toward those in power. If the attitude of the architects toward society is marked by obedience, then there is little chance of the architect gaining a critical voice. If, on the contrary, we are willing to grant architecture its own power of expression, then another perspective may come forward. What we may ask of architecture is to at least provide us with a proposition of how to see things differently, to deliver new frameworks and new interpretations. Architects should once again view their profession as part of an intellectual endeavor. For me, that is the only way in which architecture can do justice to its own potential.

3.
CASE STUDIES

Maria S. Giudici

EDUCATION, CONSUMPTION, REPRODUCTION
Three Cautionary Tales

Once upon a time, the neoliberal city was a fiction: in the nineteen-sixties, at the dawn of the knowledge economy, architects put forward projects that imagined a future beyond the Fordist paradigm—and the changed role that architecture would play in it. While at the time these fictions seemed to be simple provocations, today they have become nothing less than the reality we live in. The works of Cedric Price, Archizoom, and Superstudio[1] seem to forecast the evolution of education, consumption, and reproduction in the age of post-Fordist, neoliberal capitalism: while education finds itself at the center of the productive system, consumption becomes a social, almost political activity, and reproduction is no longer a private issue, but rather the object of statistics and economic strategy.

Over the past few years, the collective Labour City Architecture—of which Pier Vittorio Aureli and I are part—has conducted a series of studio research studies that have investigated the state of the contemporary city at the Berlage Institute, BIArch Barcelona, and the Architectural Association in London. Our theoretical premises are rooted

[1] Pier Vittorio Aureli discussed the political implications of the work of Cedric Price and, respectively, Archizoom in "Labor and Architecture: Revisiting Cedric Price's Potteries Thinkbelt," *Log* 23 (Fall 2011), and *The Project of Autonomy: Politics and Architecture within and against Capitalism* (New York: Princeton Architectural Press, 2008). Superstudio's cautionary tales are the focus of my own essay "Talking in Parables: Superstudio's Narratives," *Le Journal Spéciale'Z* 2 (Summer 2011), pp. 126–43.

in the assumptions put forward by these "cautionary tales" of the sixties (to borrow Superstudio's term): namely, that in the post-Fordist city the real object of production is no longer material goods, but rather subjectivity.[2] Subjectivity is the complex of cultural constructs, ideas, desires, and fears that shape the way people live their lives in a given historical period. Subjectivity is collective and shared; it does not refer directly to the individuals, but it does influence the way individuals perceive themselves and their environment.

The quality that sets biopower apart from traditional sovereign power is its focus on the mastering of the *bios*, the life of the subject. This fact distinguishes the architecture of mature capitalism from that of a past in which it was still chiefly a tool of representation. The projects developed by Labour City Architecture all start from the very idea of the production of subjectivity. As such, they are conscious exasperations of the biopolitical, managerial paradigm; as the cautionary tales of the sixties, they set out to further the production of subjectivity in such a blunt manner as to put into crisis the supposedly "functional" character of architecture. The strategic attempt here is to look for an architecture that renounces the pretense of solving problems and healing its dystopian condition, one that instead seeks to expose or stage this condition in all its extreme, even absurd consequences— consequences that reveal how no action, no building, no project can merely be functional but is rather always an index of a political decision. However, the actual work of our collective is very much focused on the condition of the contemporary city, where those cautionary tales seem to have become true. The issues put forward in the scenarios of the sixties have become the hallmarks of the post-Fordist, neoliberal city: the transformation of higher education into a form of industry, the collapsing of the difference between production and consumption, the transformation of architecture into an apparatus for the reproduction of suitable subjects. Universities that are factories (and vice versa), shopping malls that are places to live and work 24/7, and agglomerations of living units without social life are clearly the main ingredients of the contemporary city.

In this context, I would like to discuss the studio work that Pier Vittorio and I conducted on the city of Athens at the Berlage Institute together with Platon Issaias and Elia Zenghelis in 2011. Athens is an exemplary case of neoliberal urbanization: expanded with a series of master plans that legalized spontaneous development rather than actively steering it, Athens is a monument to laissez-faire—a key place reflecting the

---

[2]   As far as the present inquiry is concerned, key texts on the subject
        shaped by this shifted productive context are Christian Marazzi, *Capital
        and Affects: The Politics of the Language Economy* (Cambridge, MA:
        MIT Press, 2011) and Franco Berardi, *The Soul at Work* (Los Angeles:
        Semiotext(e), 2009).

conflict between the crash of the neoliberal economy and the tragedy of immigration and precarization of labor. Athens has grown through the proliferation of one building type, the *polykatoikia*, an apartment block based on a simple concrete framework of the kind exemplified by Le Corbusier as Maison Dom-Ino (→**1**). While on the one hand the overall condition is extremely fragmented and lacks a large-scale logic, the actual repetition of the same structure throughout the city enforces an extreme spatial genericness. Confronted with the impossibility of drawing large-scale master plans, we decided to propose that our students ask themselves a different question. We suggested that they tackle the actual experience of the inhabitants by formulating new typologies that would cope with a scenario which—though not socially distant from the fresco painted by Price, Archizoom, and Superstudio—lacks any readability and does not offer the citizens the possibility of awareness that those cautionary tales entailed. Actually, for us, these projects are not typologies but *archetypes*: concrete physical proposals that would eventually foster a new environment by being reiterated and repeated with variations throughout the city.

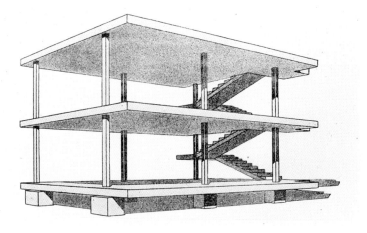

(1) Le Corbusier, Maison Dom-Ino, 1914
Source: Le Corbusier, *Oeuvre Complete*, vol. 1, 1910–29, eds. W. Boesiger and O. Stonorov (Berlin: Birkhäuser, 2006), p. 23

The core of the work pursued by Labour City Architecture is the idea of offering new narratives for a contemporary subject. This subject is no longer the factory worker belonging to a traditional family, but the precarious worker, usually linked to forms of immaterial production—a worker (or student) who lives in a highly unstable situation that has little or no political recognition. This is why we believe that in order to go beyond the neoliberal canvas it is necessary to tackle its very subject—the precarious worker—and offer this subject a form of *common*[3]: an ethos based on shared values, beyond the alienation and

[3]   We refer here to the tradition of post-operaist thinking, for instance Antonio Negri and Michael Hardt, *Commonwealth* (Cambridge, MA: Harvard University Press, 2009).

atomization suffered by the precarious worker. In fact, immaterial production, or production of knowledge, is based on exchange and communication, on sharing, a trait that offers itself as a possible beginning of new forms of solidarity. While freelance labor is unprotected and non-unionized today, this may be the right moment to imagine an alternative scenario in which the contemporary dispersion could rather foster opportunities for other kinds of social interaction, which bypass the traditional hierarchical boundaries of the family, the class, even the political party. This is the reason our proposals for Athens try to work from within instead of stepping out of the actual economic and political canvas. We accept the current condition because we believe it harbors an inherent potential, one that is latent at present but that nevertheless could be brought to light by new forms of spatial organization. Knowledge economy relies on people whose main working tool is simply language: while this means that we become less specialized in what we do, we also need to be more social. "Creativity" is one of the most abused words of the neoliberal age, precisely because it mystifies this condition by pushing the cliché that ideas are born from individuals, while they are actually the outcome of a much more collective process in which the immanent potential we all share comes to the surface and is channeled into a productive activity. Antonio Negri and Michael Hardt described the emergence of a consciousness about this "plane of immanence" as the moment in which "humans declared themselves . . . producers of cities and history"[4] at the very beginning of modernity. We believe that this is another moment where new awareness of this potential and of its collective, immanent (and not transcendental) value is called for and indeed even helped by the peculiar character of immaterial labor described above. It is also for this reason that the cautionary tales we refer to were always ambivalent toward the shifts society was undergoing: Price and Archizoom in particular felt that while we would have to leave behind the certainties of the industrial era, we would also gain other chances for cooperation and, yes, even creativity. In other words, they put forward a rudimentary architectural attempt to make what is immanent—that is, the potential embedded in the very bodies and minds of the subjects—the root of a different political and social organiza-

[4]   Michael Hardt and Antonio Negri, *Empire* (Cambridge, MA: Harvard University Press, 2001), p. 70.

tion rather than an invisible cog in the market mechanisms.[5] And the contemporary situation is still very much ambivalent: while problematic, fragmented, and exploited, we still believe that the vast layer of the population living in these precarious conditions could become the protagonist of what we call a new solidarity. As architects, our hope in dealing with Athens was precisely that sharing space could become the coagulating factor that this "immanent plane" has struggled to find up to now, remaining an extremely elusive concept. Maybe it is by going back to the acts and rituals of the everyday that it is possible to imagine forms of commonality *within and against* the neoliberal city, as the operaist leitmotif says. This entails a working method that accepts the risk of having to get its hands dirty by manipulating the city from within the mechanisms of capitalism, one piece at a time, through small interventions; a method radically opposed to the straightforward narratives posited in the cautionary tales; a method that works on the same themes indeed, but by establishing micronarratives that do not necessarily pretend to be the right answer, but only to shed light on fields of intervention that are yet undeveloped.

A key concern in our work, since we believe that knowledge is central to the contemporary city, is education—in Athens as in most Western European cities. As Cedric Price imagined in his projects Potteries Thinkbelt (1966) and Fun Palace (1961–69), education has become both a commodity and a fundamental economic engine. Potteries Thinkbelt (→**2**) was a complex for higher education that reused the industrial railroad of Staffordshire, a former center for the production of pottery which, by that time, was suffering a harsh decline. Price imagined that in the future the university would no longer be an ivory tower but rather the heart of any productive system: and, as a matter of fact, today in Europe the production of knowledge has taken the place of mechanical production that can be handled with little manpower. In the *Thinkbelt*, the industrial legacy of Staffordshire would be directly transformed into a living basis for the knowledge industry, a flexible system where architecture would be reduced to what Price referred to as "life conditioning"[6]—a way to shape and foster life. This idea recalls what would later become the orthodox Foucauldian

[5]   The more advanced the form of capitalism, the more its subjects are both harshly exploited, but also highly educated: the idea that such a condition might give rise to a different form of organization that could ultimately displace capitalism is a well-known leitmotiv of Marxist thinkers and operaists in particular, which has known a renaissance in the last few decades through the works of the so-called "post-operaists." See the already quoted *Empire* by Hardt and Negri, where the idea of solidarity goes beyond traditional Marxism and is arguably also inspired by the philosophical work of Giorgio Agamben, in particular in *The Coming Community* (Minneapolis: University of Minnesota Press, 1993).

[6]   Cedric Price, "Life-Conditioning," *Architectural Design* 36 (October 1966), pp. 483–94.

(2) Cedric Price, Potteries Think-belt, Perspective of Madeley Transfer Area, 1964–66
Source: Cedric Price, *The Square Book* (London: Wiley-Academy, 2003), p. 24

(3) Cedric Price, Sketch for the Fun Palace on the Lea Valley Site, 1964
Source: Cedric Price, *The Square Book* (London: Wiley-Academy, 2003), p. 60

definition of biopower,[7] but Price actually thought of it as a bottom-up, empowering condition.

Price also understood that production would no longer be confined to the hallowed loci of the workers' struggle—the factory, the workshop—but that it would rather happen everywhere people could meet and communicate. He explored this possibility in another project: the Fun Palace (→**3**), a complex of rehearsal and performance spaces conceived in collaboration with actress and director Joan Littlewood. In this project, Littlewood and Price address the idea of theater and performance as both a productive and a pedagogical issue. The Fun Palace would be a structure reduced to its technical components, sharing with the Thinkbelt the same link with industrial heritage turned over to culture industry. In the Fun Palace, people would perform, rehearse, and watch other spectacles in a continuum of theater and life. Although it was not realized for practical and economic reasons, it was a highly realistic project that Price and Littlewood almost managed to build. The Fun Palace tackles the idea of pedagogy through

[7]   Foucault defined biopower as the "techniques for achieving . . . the control of populations," in *The History of Sexuality*, vol. 1: *An Introduction* (1978; repr., New York: Vintage Books, 1990), p. 140.

performance: in the Palace, people would learn through experience, by mobilizing their ability to interact socially and to perform under the eyes of others—a condition that, for post-operaist thinkers like Paolo Virno,[8] is the very core of so-called immaterial production.

It is for these reasons that, while rethinking new alternatives for Athens, we decided to produce two archetypes that deal specifically with the issue of immaterial production, production of knowledge, and education. These archetypes are targeted at the production of cheap places for work and study. As a matter of fact, Price thought that the state would continue to be heavily involved in projects such as the Fun Palace or the Thinkbelt, where students would be paid to learn, since they would be understood as a valuable part of the productive process. What happened is exactly the opposite—the university has become a factory where workers pay in order to work rather than the other way around. Moreover, finding affordable space is increasingly difficult for freelance workers today. The students, the knowledge producers, and the so-called creative class in general are actually a very exploited category with no form of welfare protection.

The first archetype, the Theatre (→**4**), is precisely imagined as a welfare intervention; a concrete frame that follows the Dom-Ino principle, this skeleton is kept completely open and freely accessible. In the Theatre, the polykatoikia protocol is twisted by the introduction of staircases that build up a seamless promenade that connects top to bottom, enhancing the public character of the space. The Theatre is not literally a theater, but rather an open, covered public interior that

(4) Hyun Soo Kim, Theatre, 2011
Source: Labour City Architecture, *Athens, Towards a Common Architectural Language.* Berlage Institute Project Report, 2011

(5) Davide Sacconi, Polykatoikia 2, 2011
Source: Labour City Architecture, *Athens, Towards a Common Architectural Language.* Berlage Institute Project Report, 2011

---

[8]   An analysis of the subjectivity entailed by this condition can be found in Paolo Virno, *A Grammar of the Multitude: For an Analysis of Contemporary Forms of Life* (Los Angeles: Semiotext(e), 2004).

people can use as a space to gather and engage in various activities. As a skeleton that can be appropriated for study, rehearsal, classes, exhibitions, the Theatre is a reflection on Price's Fun Palace. While the function is the same, the architecture is low-tech as much as Price's was high-tech, underlining the fact that in a post-Fordist society the core machine is the human body. Almost archaic in its simplicity, the Theatre is a shell ready to be occupied by actions we cannot and should not predetermine, a place that fosters productive potential not immediately linked to market needs.

If the Theatre imagines a critique of the polykatoikia based on a possible acupunctural state intervention, the space called Polykatoikia 2 formulates the possibility of a new kind of private subject, a community formed by the people who own apartments in a given block. By redeveloping the empty lots and demolishing derelict buildings, the community could build a new typology on top of the current buildings, a typology that would overcome the current condition of pixelation of the built tissue (→**5**). In this way, the local inhabitants become stakeholders of the new construction that densifies the existing block. The Polykatoikia 2 is a collectively owned space that offers possibilities beyond those allowed by the current polykatoikia. It is an uninterrupted space that runs above the existing roofs, whose interior can be divided flexibly depending on individual needs, thus offering the inhabitants more space for working and enjoying leisure activities. This construction would frame the block giving it a new readability, but it would especially raise the issue of the representation of a new (freelance) working class that is today completely fragmented. All of the working and studying activities that now take place within apartments with inadequate space and little communication could have, in the Polykatoikia 2, a dignified space that also becomes a place where the surrounding cityscape may be viewed. Freelance work, which is traditionally faceless and atomized, could thus be given a place to exist and also a recognizable anatomy in relationship with the city.

Both the Theatre and the Polykatoikia 2 try to accommodate activities that do not fit into the traditional bourgeois polykatoikia apartments. The polykatoikias are a small-scale, residential version of what Rem Koolhaas has called the "typical plan"[9]: an architecture based on undifferentiated and homogeneous space, punctuated only by minimal and regular load-bearing structure, and enclosed by façades that are mere applied skins delimiting the property boundary. In a nutshell, an extreme version of the Maison Dom-Ino system. Interestingly enough, in 1969 Archizoom Associati had proposed No-Stop City, a city freed

[9]   Rem Koolhaas, "Typical Plan," in *SMLXL* (New York: Monacelli Press, 1995), pp. 334–49.

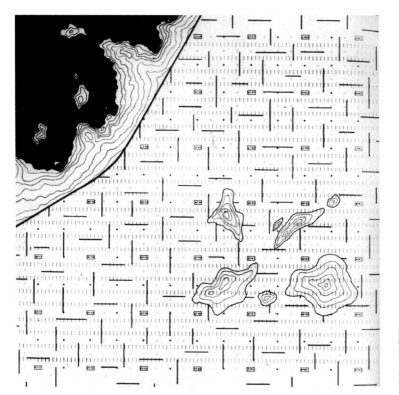

(6) Archizoom Associati, No-Stop City, 1969
Source: Andrea Branzi, *No-Stop City—Archizoom Associati* (Paris: Librairie de l'Architecture et de la Ville, 2006), p. 52

of architecture[10] which, in turn, looked like an all-encompassing typical plan or an infinite Dom-Ino (→**6**).[11] A bathroom every fifty square meters, an elevator every one hundred square meters; the city here is reduced to its most basic elements. Often perceived as provocation on paper, the project actually wanted to be an act of radical realism, and today it is clear that there is nothing utopian about it. As a matter of fact, the archetype we call the Platform (→**7**) proposes the removal of all non-load-bearing partitions at the ground floor of a given block, exposing the inherently generic structure of the Athenian tissue. The result is an uneven field of columns and cores, which is just a continuous typical plan. By tiling the resulting interior with one consistent material, the Platform would become a new covered shared space, opening up possibilities of social interaction, new local connections, and pedestrian routes. We can imagine all of the ground floors of Athens becoming Platforms and therefore demonstrating the veracity of the No-Stop City cautionary tale.

[10]   See Andrea Branzi, *No-Stop City: Archizoom Associati* (Paris: Librairie de l'Architecture et de la Ville, 2006).
[11]   Koolhaas himself says that "Archizoom interpreted Typical Plan as the terminal condition of (Western) civilization;" see "Typical Plan," p. 348.

(7) Ivan K. Nasution, Platform,
2011
Source: Labour City Architecture,
*Athens, Towards a Common
Architectural Language*. Berlage
Institute Project Report, 2011

Retail space is shrinking in central Athens, and consumption patterns are changing in unprecedented ways—e-commerce, shopping malls, and a new form of austerity are killing small-scale shops, and while this is a deadly blow to the urban intensity of inner Athens, the Platform would confront the problem by turning the unused space into another kind of condenser of activities. This transformation occurs in most twenty-first-century metropolises, as No-Stop City had already forecast. Its plan was the result of the superimposition of three typologies: the supermarket, the factory, and the parking lot. What the No-Stop City brought forward was ultimately the fall of the traditional differentiation between consumption and production in cities where the factory and the supermarket are virtually the same thing; consuming is as productive as the very act of production itself.

In Archizoom's intentions, the No-Stop City was not an entirely negative scenario: they thought that by acknowledging the blurring of boundaries, new possibilities would arise for the inhabitants of the city. In particular, they thought that by de-masking the condition of alienation in which we all live, the subjects would ultimately be empowered and that other forms of freedom and creativity would emerge. Under the disguise of a project, the No-Stop City tells the story of what is actually happening today. With the exception of few natural features or architectural preexistences, the contemporary city has actually transformed into a continuous carpet of urbanization, so much so that the No-Stop City could today be the faithful depiction of any city; however, while its basic spatial and social assumption has become true, the reality is far less readable and therefore far less "empowering." In fact, architecture has done everything it could to mask the actual sameness of the building stock we live in, inventing icons with no content, fake monuments without anything to celebrate, and clothing (with ever-changing façades) a sprawling mass of housing and offices that actually share exactly the same concrete skeleton structure.

On the other hand, Archizoom had already understood that new technologies don't necessarily drive us only toward the standardization of urban space, but also to an increasing possibility of customization of our own small-scale dwelling. Their cautionary tale therefore tells us how the consumer-producer of the neoliberal city would be able to have an increasingly personalized and customized habitat while still living in an urban condition marked by rising genericness. While this condition finds an overall framework in the schematic clarity of the No-Stop City, in reality it becomes the most problematic paradox of neoliberal urbanization, an environment where objects and infrastructure have become the crucial problems for design, while the scale of the architecture of the city undergoes a crisis. This is particularly true in Athens, where the proliferation of uncoordinated polykatoikias never allows the construction of readable, consistent urban spaces. To solve this issue, building regulations tried in the past to enforce the construction of stoas, or porticos, but never succeeded, and today these spaces are fragmented, underused, and even unsafe. This is why we believe it is necessary to rethink a different kind of Stoa archetype (→**8**). The Stoa proposes reducing the circulation space in certain main streets by adding a new freestanding colonnade in front of the existing buildings; a structure that provides visual and spatial continuity. Besides creating a public covered sidewalk, the Stoa offers the possibility of hosting new activities in the old stoas that can be appropriated as working spaces by the owners of the buildings. By creating continuity, the Stoa allows a new reading of the city structure, shields passersby from the sun, and reintroduces a bid to public space in a city that has none and that is solely left to private initiative, while providing new spaces for the inhabitants to break the mold of polykatoikias that are spatially obsolete in the face of contemporary need for flexibility.

And if we look at the inadequacy of the average Athenian apartment house, we cannot but agree with Superstudio, who, in a 1969 issue of *Domus*,[12] stated that the houses of the future would be generic

[12]   Superstudio, "Design d'evasione e d'invenzione," *Domus* 476 (1969), p. 28.

(8) Roberto Soundy, Stoa, 2011
Source: Labour City Architecture,
*Athens, Towards a Common
Architectural Language*. Berlage
Institute Project Report, 2011

structures "without surprises or hope," in a world where the quality of the environment would be set by objects instead (or a lack thereof). Two years after this bleak premonition, they published a text with images titled "Twelve Cautionary Tales for Christmas"[13] which discussed the issue of the destiny of architecture. Subtitled "Premonitions of the Mystical Rebirth of Urbanism," the text is a collection of twelve short stories that portray fictional cities of a future that might as well be a distant past, where extreme technological advancement is paralleled by a progressive reduction of human life to its biological essence. The "Cautionary Tales" describe cities that are no longer utopias, but rather selective descriptions of aspects that are already recognizable in contemporary urbanization. They depict twelve exemplary conditions with the precision of a scientific documentary, simplifying the facts of life to their minimum. In almost all of the tales, the process of reproduction is referred to in technical terms, and if there is any hint of instincts and feelings, it is under an extremely reified form: humankind has here renounced any pretense to the gratuitous, the ritual, even the festive, and can be described through its *habits* rather than its ethos.

[13]   Superstudio, "Twelve Cautionary Tales for Christmas: Premonitions of the Mystical Rebirth of Urbanism," *Architectural Design* 41, no. 12 (December 1971), pp. 737–42 and 785.

(9) Superstudio, *The City of Splendid Houses*, 1971
Source: Superstudio, "Twelve Cautionary Tales for Christmas. Premonitions of the Mystical Rebirth of Urbanism," *Architectural Design* XLI, 12 (December 1971), p. 742

Superstudio relate, in a deadpan tone, life conditions that are an extrapolation of our current reality. Up to this point, their operation has been one of absolute realism—but by singling out one aspect in each of the twelve cities, they produce a symbolic overload, with a strategy that aims at recuperating a dignity of human life from the managerial character architecture has assumed in an advanced capitalistic society. Superstudio's subjects are all reduced to "bare life,"[14] although the managerial mechanisms vary: a strict seclusion of individuals who cannot communicate ("2000-Ton City"), the possibility of living all fantasies through a simulation game ("Barnum City"), the transformation of the inhabitants into robots ("City of Order"). If there is an apparent exception to this flattening of subjectivity, it is the "City of Splendid Houses" (→**9**). In the "City of Splendid Houses" the aesthetic will of the individuals becomes the most fundamental character; while all of the buildings have the same floor plan, the inhabitants can decorate the façades to their taste, resulting in a magnificent competition of creativity. While the "City of Splendid Houses" is easily readable as a critique of consumer society, beyond the surface lies the same tale of control and genericness that informs the other cities: "all the citizens work in the city's factories," since the apparent aesthetic vitality is purely a stimulus for the production system that keeps the economy of the city afloat. Even if the apparatus varies, the citizens of all the cities have been stripped of any chance to lead a conscious life. Superstudio refuse to

[14]   A notion developed by Giorgio Agamben in *Homo Sacer: Sovereign Power and Bare Life* (Stanford: Stanford University Press, 1998).

further a history of "blood, sweat, and tears"[15] in which architecture has been reduced to a managerial tool. They refuse traditional design and introduce a project through words; a project aimed at restating an architecture that is still able to deal with the experiential and the ritual sides of human life; a project that is ultimately a form of rebellion against reification. In all of the twelve tales, Superstudio explore extreme scenarios where the house, as the place of the reproduction of the population, becomes a political problem before a functional one. And the house is definitely the locus where the subjectivity of the citizens is shaped; in contemporary Athens, as in a possible thirteenth tale, the families are pigeonholed in apartments that share only a poorly lit service core. The interaction between neighbors is, in principle, minimal, and the city blocks lack both public space and private shared courtyards that could improve the livability of the dense central neighborhoods. The whole city is composed of monad apartments and streets, with no in-betweens and few possibilities for sharing. To challenge this condition, we propose an archetype that could be inserted to densify incomplete, fragmented blocks. This typology is based on a blank wall toward the street (→**10**). If traditional polykatoikias are made of many non-load-bearing walls that subdivide apartments into purpose-specific cells, the Wall proposes just one single wall the circles the block, leaving the interior of the houses completely free. The wall is open on the ground floor to allow for pub-

(10) Yuichi Watanabe, Wall, 2011
Source: Labour City Architecture, *Athens, Towards a Common Architectural Language*. Berlage Institute Project Report, 2011

(11) Ji-Hyun Woo, Cloister, 2011
Source: Labour City Architecture, *Athens, Towards a Common Architectural Language*. Berlage Institute Project Report, 2011

[15]   The full subtitle of the Cautionary Tales is: "SUPERSTUDIO evoke twelve visions of ideal cities, the supreme achievement of twenty thousand years of civilization, blood, sweat and tears; the final haven of Man in possession of Truth, free from contradiction, equivocation and indecision; totally and for ever replete with his own PERFECTION." Superstudio, "Twelve Cautionary Tales for Christmas," p. 737.

lic activities. Between buildings it is possible to see the interior of the block that becomes a shared garden. Attached to the wall, the living units are like large balconies that open generously toward the garden. If streets today are hardly the "space of public appearance"[16] that they used to be, the wall seeks to reconstruct a form of collective agency in the space *between* the streets: the block. This tale is also extreme—it leaves the city out to instead boost the intensity of the shared garden—but, as Superstudio's ideal cities, it is so in order to demonstrate how the house has become a political issue.

Fragmentation is not only visible along the streets but also within the blocks, where leftover spaces are neglected and underused. The *Cloister* archetype (→**11**), in turn, proposes the creation of a community to manage the ground floor of a block; in this way, fences could be demolished, and the interior space used. As in the case of the Stoa, the addition of a new architectural element, a regular façade, would underline the consistency of the interior space, a space where individual owners do give up the property of the ground floor but are given back generous exterior spaces for new uses in exchange, such as spaces for freelance work and larger living rooms. Also here, the obsolete model of the polykatoikia, based on a classic nuclear family system, is questioned. By integrating new flexible spaces, the block will be able to cope with the changed needs of the inhabitants while adding some breathing space for the citizens—a new collective space which tricks the rules of a market that just offers standardized apartments that do not really fit the people who live there.

As a response to the idea of the cautionary tales becoming real, these archetypes all tackle the same conceptual category: the *common*. The common is the immanent potential present in a collection of singularities.[17] Specific, yet shared, the common has a double meaning in these projects: first of all, the possibility of sharing beyond formalized public space; and secondly, on a meta-level, the attempt to build the city in a way that blurs the opposition of public versus private and bottom-up against top-down. The projects start with the small scale of building typology but aim at influencing the readability of the city at large. This is why the end of our investigation produced one drawing that figured forth a possible scenario for Athens (→**12**). The drawing represents the application of the archetypes in different conditions; it is neither a literal portrait of Athens, nor a master plan—even be it in the form of acupuncture. It is a form of a new cautionary tale, a hopeful one, which forecasts a regeneration of the neoliberal city through

[16]   An expression that Hannah Arendt used to describe the space of politics per se in *The Human Condition* (Chicago: University of Chicago Press, 1958).

[17]   Both the concept of the *common* and the idea of the *multitude* as a political subject composed by a collection of singularities have been investigated in Negri and Hardt, *Commonwealth.*

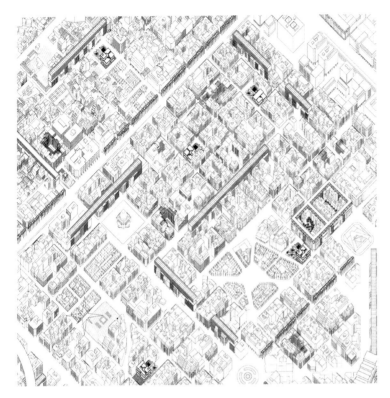

(12) Labour City Architecture collective, *Analogous Athens*, 2011 Source: Labour City Architecture, *Athens, Towards a Common Architectural Language*. Berlage Institute Project Report, 2011

archetypes that uncover the reality of the living and working condition of precarious workers. In the end, what Superstudio put forward with their architecture through storytelling was the idea that architecture is first and foremost a form of knowledge: before constructing our physical world, it constructs our common subjectivity, our shared *Weltanschauung*. This is why our project for Athens attempts to work with the neoliberal city not by inventing utopian plans, but by introducing new narratives that imagine ways of social interaction and less alienated labor. Ultimately, these narratives are all proposed through the means of space, of architecture. For us, architecture is a form of the common—the "ultimate verifiable fact," as Aldo Rossi called it,[18] and it is by conceiving architecture as a form of the common that we might, hopefully, reclaim it as a heuristic device.

[18]   Aldo Rossi, *The Architecture of the City* (New York: Oppositions Books, 1984), p. 29.

Gideon Boie (BAVO)

ARCHITECTURAL ASYMMETRIES

Three propositions about the added architectural value in the design of single-family homes in the nineteenth-century belt of Antwerp under the Land and Buildings Policy executed by the Autonomous Municipal Company for Real Estate and City Projects Antwerp (Ag Vespa)

Introduction

Questions about the existence of neoliberal architecture are generally answered by analyzing the role of emblematic architectural projects in major and highly speculative urban developments. However, admitting any direct relationship between architectural design and neoliberalism is in most cases carefully avoided. This paper argues that such hesitation results from self-protective resistance on the part of the architectural discipline. The evacuation of neoliberalism from the design field levels the path for an either opportunistic or idealistic attitude among architects. Opportunists will act as if architectural beauty were something that is indifferent to neoliberal machinations from above, while idealists immediately enter the arena of utopian speculation. In both cases, the architectural object is easily unplugged from its neoliberal other and thus detached from its production, distribution, and consumption.

The following paper is an initial, albeit incomplete, stepping stone toward the ambition of identifying neoliberalism in specific aspects of architectural production, such as practice, form, scale, material, et cetera. The production of architecture under the Land and Buildings Policy in Antwerp provides a test case for sketching a direct and complex interlinkage between architecture and neoliberalism. The design of the single-family homes in the so-called *nineteenth-century belt* of the City of Antwerp exhibits the commodification of architecture, the struggle for added architectural value, and the function of everyday architecture in city marketing. The search for neoliberal (and antineoliberal) architecture must start from these classic capitalist logics.

Object

The much-discussed architectural production under the Land and Buildings Policy by Ag Vespa, an acronym for the autonomous municipal company for real estate and city projects in Antwerp, is a prime example of urban regeneration in Belgium. In Antwerp's nineteenth-century urban cluster, the autonomous municipal company Ag Vespa has purchased a substantial number of dilapidated dwellings and free parcels of land in recent years to remarket them as desirable urban homes suitable for young families. The hope and the expectation is that this *pinpricking* will revive parts of the city currently plagued by negative social situations.

Over the past years, the Land and Buildings Policy has yielded more than one hundred single-family homes acclaimed by professional and mainstream publications for their "architectural intelligence."[1] A fundamental factor is the participation of architects identified by representative bodies in the professional sector as young, highly promising talent. The objective is for dilapidated dwellings and free parcels of land—at a disadvantage in the housing market because of their troublesome physical location—to come up with innovative design solutions. Another reason for choosing young architects is their rapid employability because of their enthusiasm and idealism.

Although the production of one hundred single-family homes is modest in absolute terms, it is nevertheless unique in the context of Belgium's traditionally liberal policy. Housing production is considered a private matter with government involvement confined to regulatory matters, except for the very limited activity in social housing. The administrative passiveness is usually compensated for by launching compulsive sensitization campaigns targeted at private builders and constructing prestigious model projects in the government real-estate portfolio. Ag Vespa personifies the Antwerp city government's entrepreneurial approach to doing something about the architectural quality of the everyday living environment.

The City of Antwerp has broken with tradition in housing policy without impairing the liberal tradition of the housing market in Belgium. The autonomous municipal company is used by the City as a vehicle to correct malfunctions in the housing market—not by imposing external regulations to the market, but, ironically, by playing its very own game (i.e. the game of the market). A market operation is set up within which a revolving fund is being used to produce and distribute architecturally valuable single-family homes. The strategic, and above all recognizable, model housing projects are developed in a cost-covering

[1]   Herman Boumans, ed., *Vooruitgangsrapport AgVespa 2011: realisaties in vastgoed en stadsprojecten* (Antwerp: Ag Vespa, 2012).

model within which any profits are used for new model projects and any losses are made good by subsidies available at the regional, federal, and/or European level (subsidies for housing policy, major conurbation policy, and regional development, respectively).

The ambiguous nature of the autonomous municipal company allows us to examine in greater depth the question of the existence of neoliberal (or anti-neoliberal) architecture. It is remarkable that the acclaimed production of architecture under the Land and Buildings Policy simultaneously denies and confirms the well-known recipes of capitalism—which we conveniently define as the ground stream of neoliberalism. Herein, we notice once again that it is not enough to say that capitalism has produced a homo economicus without adding that this man is inevitably confused.[2] The same goes for neoliberalism: although it might be a more unmediated form of capitalism, it is mystifying to present neoliberalism as a system free from internal contradiction and able to stick plainly to its ideological principles.

We will now trace the zigzag path of (anti-)neoliberal architecture by analyzing the production of the single-family homes under the Land and Buildings Policy in Antwerp following its: 1) commodification; 2) struggle for profit; and 3) universalism.

First Rule: No Architectural Quality without Commodification

Neoliberalism is generally defined as being characterized by a return to the one-sided primacy of the commodification in the way society is organized to function.[3] When applied to architectural production, commodification means that the decisive arguments in the design process are characterized by merchantability and the financial interests of the stakeholders. The motive for a design is then not so much its quality, but its return. Every design decision appears as a cost item that must be justified on the financial balance sheet. Disregarding architectural quality in an individual project would not be so bad in itself, were it not for the fact that architectural quality is part of the public interest. The fad of a client affects not only the living conditions of the person himself, but also the living quality for people living nearby and the image of the city. Former Mayor of Antwerp Patrick Janssens thus cited the architectural quality of the urban environment as a spearhead of the social reconquest of the city.[4]

The building program for single-family homes under the Land and Buildings Policy by the autonomous municipal company Ag Vespa is an

---

[2]   Immanuel Wallerstein, *Historical Capitalism with Capitalist Civilisation* (1983; repr., London: Verso, 1996), p. 18.
[3]   Ibid., pp. 11ff.
[4]   Alix Lorquet, ed., *Urban Development in Antwerp: Designing Antwerp* (Antwerp: City of Antwerp, 2012).

instrument to improve the architectural quality at the everyday street level. The production breaks away from the trend of mindless repetition of inappropriate housing models currently in evidence in the Flemish housing market. Ag Vespa provides the architect, within the contours of the design brief for single-family homes, with the latitude necessary for free experimentation. The Dodoensstraat Corner House (designed by URA, 2007) is perhaps one of the most striking results of the pronounced innovation agenda (→**1**, →**2**, →**3**). The design consists mainly of an intelligent stair solution in oriented strand board (OSB) covered with transparent plastic. The triangular spiral shape was obtained by a simple offset of the façade lines in the center of the home. The small intervention produced numerous benefits compared with the original situation of the corner house—where the stairs were positioned against the only common wall of the home. Placing the stairs in the heart of the very narrow corner house reorganizes the internal circulation and, by consequence, also the distribution of space. The most important contribution of the spiral shape lies in the reduced usage of floor space for internal circulation. The footprint of the spiral stairs is minimal and, what is more, it obviates the need for an extra system of corridors. This is because the spiral staircase offers direct access to the different rooms arranged around it. An additional quality is the value generated by experiencing the stairs. While going up and down the stairs, the user repeatedly sees the home from different perspectives, which is intensified by extra openings in the stair walls.

Interestingly, the architectural specificity and singularity of the Dodoensstraat Corner House has been made possible only through the commodification of the single-family home. The qualities of the object do not arise from a pure *not-for-profit* housing desire of an individual client. The Land and Buildings Policy is actually a real estate program organized with a revolving fund. Expenditure for purchase and alteration is treated as prefinancing that will be earned back from the sale of the buildings—possibly topped up by applicable subsidies—in order to reinvest later in a new building project. So although the design of the Dodoensstraat Corner House was not subject to a direct pursuit of profit, it was certainly subject to the accumulation necessary for the survival of the overarching investment program. Design decisions were made that weigh heaviest on the budgetary balance. Any superfluous design intervention was rejected, with the design limited to the delivery of the core. It means that the building construction was provided only with façade finishing, a useful division of space, and connecting points for technical systems (gas, water, and electricity). So it is only logical that all design effort was directed solely toward the stairs. At the same time, we see an architectural quality not based on excess in detail and ornamentation, but on a sort of ascetic formalism and contextualism. The texture of the spiral stairs derives from a rough and naked use of materials—in this instance, a compound

(1) URA, Corner House Dodoen-
straat, Antwerp, 2007
(Photo: St. Bollaert, 2007)

wood material that under normal conditions would not be used visibly.
This asceticism is also evident in the use of untreated bricks as a façade
material in other Ag Vespa designs, such as the three Lucky Bar houses
(design by Mys-Bomans and RAUM Architects, 2009) (→**5**, →**6**). Interestingly, the Lucky Bar architect based the design on a search for what
he called the basis of housing. The basis lies in creating space to meet
the user's residential needs. The arrogation of the home (covering and
furnishing, etc.) is a matter for the user and not the architect. For this
reason, the architect considered only building material that *speaks for itself* in terms of structure, usage, view, form, and texture. It is easy to boil
down the architect's motive to a rationalization of the client's financial
considerations. But it is more important to recognize how the commodification of the single-family homes in Antwerp forms a design discipline
generally acknowledged as a source of a unique architectural quality.[5]

Second Rule: Added Architectural Value Is Not for Consumption

A second rule concerns the basic feature of capitalism, namely, an
economic system that socializes costs and privatizes profits.[6] No-
where is this rule more in evidence than in real estate, where value
is generally determined not so much by the inherent properties of a
building, but by factors in the surroundings. The proximity of ame-
nities, the quality of the public space, and the creative atmosphere
in the neighborhood are external factors that outweigh the costs for
materials and labor. By so doing, the real estate market imposes a
one-sided claim on public space, while the costs are transferred to

[5]   André Loeckx, "Labo Vespa," in *The Specific and the Singular: Architecture
        in Flanders 2008–2009*, ed. Katrien, Vandermarliere (Antwerp: Flanders
        Architecture Institute, 2010), pp. 217–48.
[6]   Wallerstein, *Historical Capitalism*, pp. 45 ff.

(2) URA, Corner House Dodoen-
straat, Antwerp, 2007, staircase
(Photo: St. Bollaert, 2007)

society. Instead of privatization, it makes more sense to speak of a parasitical relationship, because the real estate market does not even need to privatize the external factors in order to utilize it as added value.[7] In the best-case scenario, private profits and public costs are balanced out via an indirect system of property tax.

The Land and Buildings Policy exemplifies a tendency that inverts the above-described principle and seeks responsibility of the private homeowner in the quality of public space in Antwerp. For example, we can see in the single-family house Veldstraat (design by Huiswerk, 2006) a large glazed-window area at street level that allows the parking of bicycles, prams, and other requisites of young families (→**7**, →**8**). At the same time, the façade-wide entry portal provides a view of residential functions on the front side of the building. Design decisions of this kind are diametrically opposed to housing tradition in Belgium, where everyday life—particularly the kitchen and the dining room—occurs in ancillary buildings at the rear of the home. Reducing the resident to an end user makes it easy for Ag Vespa to market homes that no

[7]   See Michael Hardt and Toni Negri, *Commonwealth* (Cambridge, MA:
        Belknap Press, 2009), pp. 153–57.

longer turn away from public space but generously open up toward it. The result is public space with a high value of experience, according to the goal defined by the Chief City Architect of Antwerp, Kristiaan Borret.[8] In this respect, the Land and Buildings Policy privatizes the cost item of architectural quality (the housing paid for by the consumer) and socializes its added value (which the anonymous passerby enjoys). Nevertheless, the added architectural value of the Land and Buildings Policy is still being privatized in a rather unexpected way. The upgrading of the street's liveability is maximized by selecting parcels of land and dilapidated buildings at carefully chosen places in the neighborhood. One could thus frame the privatization of added architectural value in terms of the user who is given the privilege of living in the most desirable parts of the street. However, from the consumer's perspective the profit is limited, because he or she is obliged to make alterations to the delivered core before it attains usefulness. It is symptomatic that the architectural interventions in the Dodoensstraat Corner House turned out to have no value whatsoever for the consumer.

(3) URA, Corner House Dodoen-straat, Antwerp, 2007, interior view (Photo: St. Bollaert, 2007)

(4) URA, Corner House Dodoen-straat, Antwerp, 2007, interior view after closing off the openings in the spiral stairs (Photo: St. Bollaert, 2007)

[8]   Kristiaan Borret, *Beleidsnota Stadsbouwmeester 2006–2011* (Antwerp: City of Antwerp, 2007).

(5) Mys & Bomans and RAUM,
House Oudemansstraat-Keistraat
(Lucky Bar), Antwerp, 2009
(Photo: N. Donckers, 2009)

(6) Mys & Bomans and RAUM,
House Oudemansstraat-Keistraat
(Lucky Bar), Antwerp, 2009, inte-
rior view of an apartment
(Photo: N. Donckers, 2009)

The new owner was not a family, but a single person who uses the building as a private home with bed-and-breakfast facilities. For this purpose, the owner reorganized the minimal distribution of space and closed off the openings in the spiral stairs (→**4**). To no avail, he even made some attempts to paint over the OSB, which failed because of the plastic treatment of the OSB. Privatization on the part of the consumer is outweighed by the double costs that he or she must bear for the purchase and the necessary alterations.

The main privatization of added architectural value in the Land and Buildings Policy is to be located at the side of the distributor, i.e., the autonomous municipal company Ag Vespa. The specific choice for targeting corner houses is not so much inspired by the privileged position as it is by the visibility of the objects. Corner houses are not favourite items in the housing market as they lack some elements that are regarded fundamental to the Belgian housing culture, such as rear windows, gardens,

(7) Bovenbouw (formerly known as Huiswerk), House Veldstraat, Antwerp, 2006
(Photo: Van Eetveldt Nyhuis Photography, 2006)

ancillary buildings, etc. However, corner houses are welcome objects because they are situated along several lines of sight and thus generate maximum impact on the local community. Within Ag Vespa's business model, the omnipresence of the single-family homes in the neighborhood has diverse benefits. Firstly, the single-family homes function as icons of the professional city management that the parent company, namely the City of Antwerp, has introduced to end the political games and corruption under the previous mayors. Secondly, the single-family homes function as a market tool to seduce young families to settle in the impoverished nineteenth-century belt of the city. Thirdly, the single-family homes function as an exemplary project in the sensitization of the local residents to take up responsibility for their living environment. In short, while the expenditure on architectural quality is billed to the housing consumer, the quality only has significance and value for the distributor of the objects. The parasitical relation continues and even intensifies after the transaction. At the moment the housing consumer moves in, the building ceases to be a mere symbol—endlessly reproduced in magazines—and effectively becomes a *living structure* that communicates with the spectator.

(8) Bovenbouw (formerly known as Huiswerk), House Veldstraat, Antwerp, 2006, interior view (Photo: Van Eetveldt Nyhuis Photography, 2006)

Third Rule: City Marketing Exploits Architecture of the Everyday

The third rule concerns the need of the neoliberal system for an ideological, universal framework that provides a place in the accumulation process for all share- and stakeholders.[9] The concurrency between cities and urban regions functions today as a decisive framework for the production of an endless stream of emblematic architectural projects designed by a worldwide army of starchitects. It is universal because every city that does not engage in the urban competition lags behind inevitably. Since Frank O. Gehry's design of the Guggenheim Museum in Bilbao, having a high-profile building developed by an architect with an equally high-profile name has become a central element in the vision of the future of any self-respecting city. Besides being a marketing product, emblematic architecture has a leveraging role for urban-development projects. A landmark architectural icon

[9]   Wallerstein, *Historical Capitalism*, pp. 73ff.

guarantees public awareness of the development area and the essential investment funds.[10]

In Antwerp, Museum aan de Stroom or MAS (design by Neutelings Riedijk Architects, 2000, opened in 2011) functions as an object of city marketing and leverage of the development of the old port area called Eilandje (→**9**). Remarkably, even while it was being constructed, the reason for the existence of the museum was called into question, because it was unclear which collection would be housed in the immense building and what its financial viability would be. But the unclear use value of the building did not hamper the perspective for development of the area—just the opposite. Right from the discussion about the protracted construction, the eccentric form experiment of MAS did what it was meant to do: it functioned as a sublime and tower-high landmark for the Eilandje development area.

The difference between MAS and the production of architecture under the Land and Buildings Policy could not be greater at first sight. In the latter, there are no overheated ambitions for a disused development area. On the contrary, it is an alternative and widely supported urban renewal operation in districts of the city that have been starved of attention and investment for many years. Most projects in the Land and Buildings Policy exhibit a façade structure, building envelope, and choice of construction material that carefully simulate nearby buildings in a contemporary embodiment—such as the three-house project Gravinstraat-Gijselsstraat (design by De Smet Vermeulen architecten, 2011) (→**10**, →**11**). The limited logo value is inversely proportional to the use value of the single-family homes. First and foremost, the single-family homes meet (at least in principle) the intimate housing desires of young families and the desire among local residents for a livable street; not to forget the authentic design pleasure among the architects involved—the producers that are not usually mentioned in Ag Vespa's communications. So the single-family homes are not intended as objects of desire for the remote and restless gazes of tourists walking around the city, but as a backdrop to the day-to-day comings and goings of the local residents.

The no-logo strategy that underlies architectural production in the Land and Buildings Policy nevertheless embodies a unique and priceless value in the public relations of Antwerp. Former Mayor Patrick Janssens—who built a career for himself as a communications expert—made clear more than once that, above all, the city must win the hearts of its own residents. The central idea is that residents who identify themselves with their city will have a stronger appeal to outsiders than any public-relations campaign. The single-family homes

[10]   Erik Swyngedouw, "A New Urbanity? The Ambiguous Politics of Large-Scale Urban Development Projects in European Cities," in *Amsterdam Zuidas European Space*, ed. W. Salet (Rotterdam: 010 Publishers, 2005), pp. 61–79.

(9) Neutelings Riedijk Architects, MAS, Antwerp, 2000–11 (Photo: F. Vercruysse, 2011)

of Ag Vespa fit into this model of what we call internal city market-ing: the single-family homes formulate small, obvious messages that, unconsciously, convince local residents of a positive city project. This has been done successfully: while MAS has been snowed under with cynical reactions and will be embraced by the citizens of Antwerp only over the course of years, the Land and Buildings Policy can bank on general appreciation and spontaneous acceptance. The immedi-ate well-being of Antwerp residents is many times more effective as public-relations material than any kind of eye-catcher, which will often quickly lose its contemporary gloss and/or will be trumped by a ri-val design. Gazing into intimate, cozy interiors conveys a unique logo value: the daily presence and activity of the residents provide a scene of people who enjoy the good city life in Antwerp. The universal logic of competition based on the strategic placement of eccentric objects is thus replaced by spontaneous identification with a recognizable situation.

Balance

The material above examined Ag Vespa's architectural production based on three fundamental pillars of capitalism. Although the pillars have a knock-on effect in neoliberalism (and thus suggest themselves as points of departure when analyzing the relationship between archi-tecture and neoliberalism), we recognize that we have not elaborated

(10) Henk De Smet and
Paul Vermeulen, Three Houses
Gravinstraat-Gijselsstraat,
Antwerp, 2011
(Photo: B. Gosselin, 2011)

(11) Henk De Smet and
Paul Vermeulen, Three Houses
Gravinstraat-Gijselsstraat,
Antwerp, 2011, interior view
(Photo: B. Gosselin, 2011)

some customary themes from the literature on neoliberalism, such as restoration of class power, unequal urban developments, and neoliberal state intervention.[11]

We can merely remark here that Ag Vespa's pinpricking architectural production deserves further discussion based on these themes. It is difficult not to see the function of the single-family homes in Antwerp in the redistribution of urban space toward the white middle class. If there is one thing the neighborhoods in the nineteenth-century belt of Antwerp do not lack, it is the presence of families—however, a lot of them have a foreign background and/or live in overcrowded houses.

[11]   See David Harvey, *A Brief History of Neoliberalism* (Oxford: Oxford University Press, 2005).

At the same time, the single-family homes cannot hide the disparity between the light investment scheme for the nineteenth-century belt and the massive construction works in the old port area—with the already mentioned MAS, apartment buildings (Diener & Diener and David Chipperfield, among others), Port House (Zaha Hadid), and Antwerp Port Coördination Centre (Neutelings-Riedijk). Finally, the merging of government and market initiatives in the autonomous municipal company Ag Vespa is symptomatic for the unacknowledged hand of the state in both speculative urban developments and small-scale interventions.

The question regarding (anti-)neoliberal architecture deserves an answer that disregards the leftist myth of the internally coherent totalitarian system, which exploits every human faculty to maximize financial profit. I have described here how Ag Vespa's working method places commodification, struggle for added value, and city marketing in the light of an accumulation of architectural quality in Antwerp. Ag Vespa's single-family homes are at once speculative objects in social engineering and a sincere answer to the desires of local residents. The ambiguous design brief gives the Ag Vespa project leaders—most of whom are qualified architects—and the young architects the feeling of working together on an enterprise with the noble goal of improving the quality of the living environment. This also explains the willingness among the architects to deliver quality despite the underpaid working conditions offered by Ag Vespa. It would be wrong to assert in this context that Ag Vespa's architectural production is subject to a neoliberal apparatus—as if architecture had its own subjectivity. An apparatus is an operating network of institutions, measures, knowledge bodies, and practices that shape the behavior of a human being.[12] The architectural design is not the resulting subject, but a full-fledged part of the apparatus. Instead of subjection, we refer to a kind of self-integration; the commodification of architecture and other capitalist strategies are spontaneously applied by those involved as a condition of possibility for the thing hoped for—that is, the enjoyment of architectural quality. The resultant exclusion of the user from the design process in formal and informal public-private partnerships is seen as natural part of the professional architectural culture of Antwerp. Awaiting the further identification of neoliberal architecture within the Land and Buildings Policy, the search for anti-neoliberal architecture starts with this Gordian knot.

[12]   See Giorgio Agamben, *What Is an Apparatus?* (Stanford: Stanford University Press, 2009), pp. 1–24.

Ana Llorente

NEOLIBERAL LIAISONS
**Interactions between Architecture and Fashion
in the Age of Creative Industries**

In 2006, Nigel Coates asserted that "architecture could learn more from clothing."[1] Arising from the observation of John Galliano's work on one of the plans for a building by Branson Coates Architecture, this statement was published in *Architextiles AD*, edited by Mark Garcia, coinciding with the homonymous research project developed at the Royal College of Art, London.[2] The special issue confirmed that, decades after Frei Otto's pioneering work with lightweight tensile and membrane structures, the equation formed by architecture and textiles was becoming a relevant matter of practice and theorization, from the basis of a demand of flexibility, adaptation, and responsiveness in construction. Within this context, digital design technologies and advanced computing in textile engineering have implemented what Lars Spuybroek called the "textile way of thinking"[3]; an unexpected evolution of Gottfried Semper's *Bekleidungstheorie* (Theory of Dressing) through the transfer of tectonic properties to fabrics that seems to have relocated new fields of encounters between architecture and dress.[4]

[1]   Nigel Coates, "Skin/Weave/Pattern," in "Architextiles," ed. Mark Garcia, special
        issue, *Architectural Design* 76, no. 6 (November–December 2006), p. 48.
[2]   This program, led by Mark Garcia and Anne Toomey, basically explored
        the potential of the direct collaboration between architects and textile
        designers through the development of large-scale interventions.
[3]   See Maria Ludovica Tramontin, "Textile Tectonics: An Interview with
        Lars Spuybroek," in "Architextiles," pp. 52–59.
[4]   In 1988, Günther Feuerstein already coined the term "archi-tex-ture" to desig-
        nate the use of fabric and textile manufacturing processes in building, pointing
        out that this was an essential fact that would confirm an obvious relationship
        between architecture and dress. See Günther Feuerstein, "Editorial," in "Archi-
        textur/Architexture," special issue, *Daidalos* 29 (September 15, 1988), p. 17.

Coincidentally, two exhibitions in 2006 highlighted the interest in this connection. The Center for Architecture in New York inaugurated the year with *The Fashion of Architecture: CONSTRUCTING the Architecture of Fashion*. Months later, the itinerant exhibition *Skin + Bones: Parallel Practices in Fashion and Architecture* opened at the Museum of Contemporary Art, Los Angeles (MOCA), bringing together a wide range of contemporary names from both fields in an exploration of common places through material, conceptual, technical, and formal nexus—some of them, like wrapping or pleating, directly related to that "textile way of thinking." As these curatorial approaches showed, the examination of the relationship between architecture and clothing has strongly reemerged, however, it is scrutinized from different points of view that are inevitably imbued again by reflection on the most controversial but crucial vertex of these interwoven dimensions: fashion.[5]

This primarily social form has always been conversing with other design and artistic languages, with inspiration and collaboration as principal mediums of a search for cultural and creative recognition. Since the late nineteenth century, some of the dialogues were born from permeable grounds like avant-garde movements, as well as from a spirit of rejection against contemporary trends and the rise of industrialization in clothing production (e.g., artistic dress reform). However, the current cross-disciplinary frame of postindustrialism has allowed fashion to finally find a real effective means with which to restructure these relationships without contradicting the essence of its system, showing more than before to what extent its creative and conceptual influence could affect the nature of other languages. Within this framework, the current interactions between fashion and architecture represent a brand renewal of a phenomenon that is achieving increasing and complex amplitude.

The conjunction of the notable expansion of fashion retail, the technological advances in architectural design, and the increasing use of fabrics and clothing rhetoric in construction are articulating common concerns for both fields as creative sectors. Thus, it is necessary to analyze

[5]   A growing number of exhibitions alongside academic research programs have continued with this exploration. Nevertheless, the precedents dated back to 1982, when the Massachusetts Institute of Technology showcased *Intimate Architecture: Contemporary Clothing Design*. Several studies of the dialogues that architecture had historically established with fashion proliferated during the nineties. The group of seminars held at the Princeton University School of Architecture was remarkable, finally joined together by Deborah Fausch and Paulette Singley within their extraordinary reader. See Deborah Fausch et al., eds., *Architecture: In Fashion* (New York: Princeton Architectural Press, 1994). In parallel, Mark Wigley analyzed how, despite its spirit of rejection, modern architecture depended on fashion for its own definition. See Mark Wigley, *White Walls, Designer Dresses: The Fashioning of Modern Architecture* (Cambridge, MA: MIT Press, 1995). It was for good reason that these reviews coincided with the well-deserved establishment of Fashion Studies in academics.

the conceptual implications of dialogues that are hatching out into a type of architecture that fulfills a metamorphosis in the tireless process of fashion image-making. Although concepts such as shelter and identity, metaphoric discursive tools, and terms like hybridization have been widely used in order to shed light on this subject, the extensive presence of the fashion iconophilia in our visual urban culture also reveals how architecture is wickedly participating in the sacralization of ephemeral values—establishing neoliberal conditions such as competitiveness, precariousness, and nomadism through the apparent exploration of celebrated properties like overexposure, flexibility, or mobility.

The Fashion Consciousness

Fashion is a valuable source for decoding its time—being a system of production and distribution of a creative capital that communicates social distinction, displays wealth, or reveals necessity while constructing and reconstructing gender and defining identities. Despite this, it has been underestimated in intellectual, cultural, and creative terms.[6] Even long before the birth of its modern system,[7] fashion had been morally condemned by discourses that already criticized ephemeral, artificial, and frivolous clothing styles. After the Industrial Revolution, economic and social theories established the idea of fashion as the production of meaning through dress in society, but also as a sort of consciousness with its own rules.[8] Nevertheless, one of the main roots of criticism has lain in the logic of its system, based on the consummation of sartorial change through a deliberate disabling of the garment for the sake of a unidirectional, but reversible, trend. As sociologist Oscar Scopa would say, fashion is "empty space in the continuity of the change from an object that is degraded prior to being worn."[9]

[6] The fashion historian Valerie Steele, director and chief curator of The Museum at the Fashion Institute of Technology (FIT) in New York, wisely referred to this field as the "'F' Word" in an autobiographical account of the reactions of academics when she was working on her dissertation at Yale. See Valerie Steele, "The 'F' Word," *Lingua Franca* 1, no. 4 (April 1991), pp. 16–20.

[7] The final abolition of sumptuary laws in 1793 by the French National Convention is considered the point of departure of the modern fashion system. See Lourdes Cerrillo Rubio, *La moda moderna. Génesis de un arte nuevo* (Madrid: Siruela, 2010).

[8] The two important references of these fundaments are, first, Thorstein Veblen's "Theory of the Leisure Class" (1899) and the "conspicuous consumption" of the North American upper middle class and, second, Georg Simmel's essay "Fashion," first published in 1895.

[9] Translated from the Spanish: "ese espacio vacío de la continuidad del cambio a partir de un objeto que se degrada antes de que se desgaste." Oscar Scopa, *Nostálgicos de la aristocracia: El siglo XX a través de la moda, el arte y la sociedad* (Madrid: Taller de Mario Muchnik, 2005), p. 31.

This mechanism inherent to its structure has transcended the boundaries of this field, making fashion become a plural term extendable and applicable to other sectors—specially creative, but also social, intellectual, or even economic ones—likely to operate through a temporal succession of formal, behavioral, or structural sequences. Besides, due to that essential emptiness, generated in the mere game with social and individual drives (sometimes primitives, as Adolf Loos supported), areas like architecture have adopted a critical attitude toward fashion when they have felt the spreading *threat* of this word, reducing it to a domestic and ornamental (superficial) function and, likewise, to an irrational futility linked to gender connotations already explored by theorists like Beatriz Colomina and Mary McLeod. Fashion consciousness would become that "unprecedented illness," as Heinrich Hübsch claimed, contaminating both dress and building.[10] Only those dialogues that have served the aesthetic concerns of architecture—in fact, generally nullifying fashion's nature by the defense of timeless designs—have been recognized and fostered.

However, the in-vogue conciliation between architecture and fashion is unveiling an essential dimension of the latter: its affinity with capitalism's own consciousness. Luc Boltanski and Eve Chiapello have analyzed how capitalism neutralizes every critical response by strengthening its devices and changing its order.[11] Considered a near relation of this economic system, not only does fashion operate through very similar mechanisms of adaptation in a strategically synchronic way, it easily undermines critical currents, even encompassing those devices from which negative voices emerge. After all, it has managed to softly extend its form, provoking, as Gilles Lipovetsky has noted, "the advent of a society restructured from top to bottom by the attractive and the ephemeral—by the very logic of fashion."[12] Ultimately, every censorious thought would materialize the extent of its consciousness: "They fulminate against fashion, but they are quick to follow its lead, adopting similar hyperbolic techniques."[13] Thus, architectural rejection of fashion may finally turn into fashion. As Mark Wigley has pointed out referring to the modern movement, "antifashion fashion holds a unique grip on architectural discourse."[14]

Moreover, in the last two decades, late capitalism has set up a new socioeconomic model, in which fashion has found an ally to extend its logic: the creative industries. Spreading from the Anglo-Saxon con-

[10]   Mary McLeod, "Undressing Architecture: Fashion, Gender and Modernity," in Fausch et al., *Architecture: In Fashion*, p. 49.
[11]   Luc Boltanski and Eve Chiapello, *The New Spirit of Capitalism,* translated by Gregory Elliott (London and New York: Verso, 2007), pp. 96–9, 169–342.
[12]   Gilles Lipovetsky, *The Empire of Fashion: Dressing Modern Democracy* (New Jersey: Princeton University Press, 2002), p. 5.
[13]   Ibid., p. 9.
[14]   Wigley, *White Walls, Designer Dresses*, p. 125.

text, this frame—based on networking for the purpose of facilitating development and attaining economic benefits through innovation—has promoted patterns of interrelationship between different mediums and practices.[15] Consequently, as a system already configured by diverse agents—from textile and pattern engineers and clothing designers, to mass media professionals—fashion is operating more comfortably than ever within new spaces of encounters in which a relevant engagement with architecture has been taking place. From the increasing development of great multinational holding companies and fashion retailers' expansion, especially across Asia, architectural design has become an effective collaborator for this market colonialism with a crucial function in the establishment of brand identities. These connections also seem to promote closer partnerships that sometimes flirt with other systems. For instance, in tandem Zaha Hadid and Karl Lagerfeld conceived the Mobile Art Pavilion (2008–10) as a way to foster the artistic recognition of Chanel's design for the iconic bag called *2:55*. Beyond public policies related to promoting creative sectors, this basis endorses a capitalist architecture that would have taken a prominent position at the forefront of fashion image-making.[16] For a good understanding of this process, it is necessary to point out that, after structural changes caused by the democratization of luxury, since the second half of the twentieth century the fashion industry has inserted its system into an iconophile process. The strength of the image as fetish and the power of the firm as symbol of corporative and social distinction have pushed the garment into a secondary role for the definition and even consumption of fashion: "Current fashion participates in an economic system that is developing very differently from its nineteenth-century origins, which pioneered the techniques of retail and advertising to promote the garment. Now the fashioned garment circulates in a contemporary economy as part of a network of signs, of which the actual garment is but one."[17]

[15]   For a deep analysis of the organization of the creative industries, see Richard E. Caves, *Creative Industries: Contracts between Art and Commerce* (Cambridge, MA: Harvard University Press, 2001); John Hartley, ed., *Creative Industries* (Cambridge, MA, and Oxford: Blackwell Publishing, 2005); and Paul Stoneman, *Soft Innovation: Economics, Product Aesthetics, and the Creative Industries* (Oxford: Oxford University Press, 2010).

[16]   As Tom Dyckhoff said on behalf of *Skin + Bones*: "Despite appearances to the contrary (black polo necks, black suits, black round Corbusier spectacles, black shoes offset with one luridly neon element), architects are as fashion-conscious as regular human beings." Tom Dyckhoff, "Heights of fashion in the world of architecture: Gehry to Koolhaas," *The Times*, February 23, 2008, http://www.thetimes.co.uk/tto/arts/visualarts/architecture/article1887497.ece (accessed June 2010).

[17]   Caroline Evans, "Yesterday's Emblems and Tomorrow's Commodities," in *Fashion Cultures: Theories, Explorations and Analysis*, eds. Stella Bruzzi and Pamela Church Gibson (London and New York: Routledge, 2006), p. 96.

Un PORTFOLIO de VOGUE à l'usage des ÉLÉGANTES

(1) *Un portfolio de VOGUE à l'usage des ÉLÉGANTS*,
Vogue, February-March, 1948,
Maison Balenciaga, 10, Avenue
George V, Paris
Source: Leslie Ellis Miller, *Balenciaga* (Barcelona: Editorial Gustavo Gili, 2007)

What is more, the spaces for sale, display, and consumption have shifted from a real to a virtual condition, leading to what Caroline Evans has called the "deterritorialization" of the garment[18]—an outlook that has consequently reconfigured traditional functions for retail architecture.

In a report for *Vogue*, published in 1948 and referred to by Lesley Miller in her study of Balenciaga's commercial strategy,[19] the most important Parisian maisons couture were located in the new map of

[18]   Ibid.
[19]   Lesley Ellis Miller, *Balenciaga* (Barcelona: Gustavo Gili, 2007), p. 61.

(2) Herzog & de Meuron, Prada Store, Aoyama, Tokyo, 2003 (Photo: Patrick Collins)

(3) Kumiko Inui, Dior Flagship *Store*, Ginza Shopping District, Tokyo, 2004 (Photo: Luis Villa del Campo)

Peltier, stressing the importance of their placement in the city. As seen in the photograph, the emblematic 10th Avenue George V, built in 1887, is merely marked by the Balenciaga name, a sign of a soft "commercial colonialism" (→**1**). This subtle occupation of the city by fashion is nowadays kept within traditional shopping districts, like the Golden Mile in Madrid or the Golden Triangle in Paris, generating relationships of harmonic coexistence between the major luxury brands. In this regard, it should be noted the same soft integration has spread across representative areas of certain firms through practices of restoration and occupation of landmark buildings. An extreme case is represented by the multinational group Inditex, with emblematic acquisitions for Zara's megastores like the old cinema at Corso Vittorio Emanuele II in Milan, the convent of San Antonio el Real in Salamanca, or emblematic buildings on the Champs-Élysées in Paris. This practice of architectural disguise poses a sort of simulacrum of distinction by a sector of the fashion industry fed by the production of cheap emulations of the designs of luxury brands.

Nevertheless, though still being the primary form for placing fashion commodities within the city, attending to the iconic nature of new stores, there is a shift from the idea of the shop as mainly a physical retail space to an architectural embodiment of the brand's products. Taking a look at avant-garde shopping districts in Tokyo, the metamorphosis is revealed by stores like Louis Vuitton (Jun Aoki, 2002), Prada (Herzog & de Meuron, 2003 (→ **2**), Dior (SANAA, 2003), or Tod's

(Toyo Ito, 2004). These signature buildings use spectacular visibility as global capitalist language that avoids any possible *lost in translation* in marketing communication. But most of them also articulate visual codes explicitly related to the luxury brands' style and products. For instance, the play of light and transparency of the delicate acrylic curtain of the Dior flagship store in Omotesando, Tokyo, is as evocative of the creative universe of the French house as the double skins created by Kumiko Inui for its various buildings—in Osaka (2005), Nagoya (2007) or Tokyo's Ginza district (2004)—which adresses Dior's original Carnage stitching pattern (→**3**).

Hélène Lipstadt has analyzed architecture and *haute couture* as systems that function with similar operations between the economic and the symbolic fields, and grant the value of their objects by means of style and signature.[20] After all, both spheres of creation could be viewed as "battlefields," so to speak, "where competition for resources and status forms part of its central dynamic."[21] This proximity is consummated through the natural immersion of the architect's design into the fashion's firm, providing the store with the distinctive image of a brand commodity and not only of his own signature building. Thus, those spaces for sale establish among them relationships of status competition based on differentiation, transforming the urban spaces into jungles inhabited by *fashion-conscious artifacts* fighting in a sort of commercial "post-evolutionary panorama."

The Textile Consciousness

The phenomenon described acquires further connotations considering the application of the "textile way of thinking" in building. The material quality of the real or simulated fabric applied to any typology engenders ideas such as connectivity, flow, flexibility, or mobility and, consequently, it could carry out a perfect architectural metaphor of the kind of social interactions which characterized the neoliberal context. For instance, taking Shigeru Ban's emblematic Curtain Wall House (Tokyo, 1995) as a model of interconnection of the public and private spheres of life due to the mobile architectural element, a textile formulation turns out to be a good solution for the creative labor class in dealing with the social isolation caused when their home is also their working place (→**4**). Despite using an exterior curtain for a transparent façade rather than a direct textile curtain wall, Maria Flöckner and Hermann Schnöll have designed a similar flexible solution in 47°40'48"n/13°8'12"e house (2007). Conceiving their project as a model of adaptation to other locations, the architects have also

[20]   Fausch et al., *Architecture: In Fashion*, pp. 14–5.
[21]   Nick Ryan, "Prada and the Art of Patronage," *Fashion Theory Journal* 11, no. 1 (2007), p. 13.

(4) Shigeru Ban, Curtain Wall House, Tokyo, 1995
(Photo: Hiroyuki Hirai)

(5) Maria Flöckner and Hermann Schnöll, House 47°40'48"n/13°8'12"e, Salzburg, 2007
(Photo: Stephan Zenzmaier)

pointed out the importance of contemporary geographical mobility (→**5**). The extreme transparency of the façade creates an openness that seems to nullify the idea of the building as a solid and well-defined property, and it is reminiscent of the "universal floor" of Shigeru Ban's Wall-Less House (Nagano, 1997). Fitting in some way with that "location that has no location,"[22] it has been planned as an "extension of both the vectoral streetscape and the visual landscape (or surroundings)"; it is "merely a hub in a personal network"[23] that can be mounted for any environment. Indeed, the façade only turns visible when the curtain is opened around, which outlines the attachment to a symbolical definition of a portable structure.

The use of textile allusions inevitably evokes archetypical transient constructions, extrapolating this reminiscence to a new and (mostly) fatal nomadic age—sweetened by globalization, which features it as a positive condition persuading the docile acceptance of an economically precarious life that usually leads to migration.[24] Taking Isabell Lorey's idea of "biopolitical governmentality and self-precarization" in order to examine the very power of the creative industries in this regard, Gerald Raunig noted: "Is the creative industry . . . a system that enslaves its subjects, or is there a specific form of involvement of the actors within this process of precarization? . . . what is changing here, according to Isabell Lorey's argument, is the *function* of precarization: from an immanent contradiction in liberal governmentality to a function of normalization in neoliberal governmentality."[25]

This condition has given rise to creative responses that use the interaction between architecture and clothing for the representation of portable habitations in order to articulate conceptual reflections on contemporary determinisms regarding space, migration, and isolation. Fashion designer Hussein Chalayan's *Afterwords* (S/S 2000) or Lucy Orta's *Refuge Wear* (→**6**) work on this line: "Today's world is marked by an extreme fragility and precariousness. No one can be spared. The fall, with no safety net at the bottom . . . Deprived of work, money, shelter, the third world is gradually invading the major capitals."[26]

[22]   Paul Virilio, "The Overexposed City," in *The Paul Virilio Reader*, ed. Stephen Redhead (New York: Columbia University Press, 2004), p. 91.

[23]   The project 47°40'48"n/13°8'12"e house, website of Maria Flöckner and Hermann Schnöll, http://www.floecknerschnoell.com/architektur/projekte/474048n130812e/english.html (accessed November 2011).

[24]   By specifying the location through the name of the house—47°40'48"n/13°8'12"e—would not an intimate need of a place be expressed?

[25]   Gerald Raunig, "Creative Industries as Mass Deception," trans. Aileen Derieg, European Institute for Progressive Cultural Policies, January 2007, http://eipcp.net/transversal/0207/raunig/en (accessed September 2011).

[26]   Jerome Sans in "Orta Artwork," website of Studio-Orta, http://www.studio-orta.com/artwork_fiche.php?fk=&fs=1&fm=0&fd=0&of=1 (accessed March 2012).

(6) Lucy Orta, *Refuge Wear Installation,* Le Cité de Refuge, Salvation Army, Paris, 1995
Source: http://www.studio-orta.com

On the contrary, the textile logic applied to fashion stores could adopt an inverse meaning when it serves to metonymic representations of a brand's products: what should be flexible and portable becomes firm and static. This is what has happened in the model case of Louis Vuitton and the unequivocal architectural encoding of its identity. Jun Aoki's work for some of Vuitton's most distinctive stores plays, through different effects, with the envelopes in order to dress the building with iconic patterns of the French luxury label, as would be the case with the aforementioned architectural designs by Kumiko Inui for Dior. One of the first examples of this visual strategy is its Louis Vuitton building in Nagoya (1999), where a double skin reproduces a well-studied moiré effect with the repetition of the patterns on which the firm based the *Monogram and Damier Canvas* series (→**7**).[27] The architectural design provides, through the solidity of the building, a code of stability for fashion consumption that symbolically nullifies the temporality of the products, giving a principle of eternity to the label. Even more, the typology of the stores is reconfigured to achieve a consistent loyalty not only to the brand but to the commodity that is represented by the same building, establishing clever relations of analogy that produce wise turns and conceptual revisions of Semper's Theory of Dressing.

(7) Jun Aoki, Louis Vuitton Boutique, Nagoya, Tokyo, 1999
Source: http://www.flickr.com/photos/colbwt-archi/2911078631/

(8) Takashi Murakami, temporal façade for Louis Vuitton Store, New York, 2008–09
Source: http://www.flickr.com/photos/nyclovesnyc/3103001963/sizes/l/in/photostream/

[27]   The building can be seen as a truthful image of the interior spaces. This would turn a radical embodiment of the mechanisms of fashion into that paradigm of the operation of the code noticed by Jean Baudrillard. See Xavier Puig Peñalosa, *La crisis de la representación en la era postmoderna: el caso de Jean Baudrillard* (Quito: Abya-Yala, 2000).

The Clothing Experience

Entering these iconic landmark buildings fosters a feeling of being fashionable, thus accomplishing the symbolic experience of being dressed with them. After all, as Wigley states on behalf of Semper's theories, buildings "are worn rather that simply occupied."[28] As a convergent experience, Karen A. Frank would raise the question: "Is it not possible that 'wearing' the building, even as a one-time, can stimulate similar feelings?"[29] Upon entering, the store acquires its realization as an artifact and, at last, as a material commodity, allowing a type of "pre-consumption" from the fetish involvement in spaces focused not on Charles Baudelaire's *flâneur* but on the new "interactive citizen-consumers" that the creative industries address.[30] Once there, these boutiques would slightly commit us to certain transformations of our appearance, persuading the potential costumer to recreate one's self-image in order to satisfy the necessity of being "on the guest list" in terms of consumerism.[31] Even the interiors could critically exceed playing with fashion promises of renewal and fulfillment, as happens at the *commercial panopticon* that Kramdesign has disposed at the Prada flagship store in New York (Rem Koolhaas, 2001). A technological environment deploys screens showing models at the catwalk, alongside images of the customers that are recorded and privately shown by the mirrors inside the dressing rooms.[32]

[28]   Wigley, *White Walls, Designer Dresses*, p. 12.
[29]   Karen A. Frank, "Yes, We Wear Buildings," in "Fashion + Architecture," ed. Helen Castle, special issue, *AD Architectural Design* 70 no. 6 (2000), p. 96.
[30]   Hartley, *Creative Industries*, p. 5.
[31]   Angela McRobbie, "Clubs to Companies," in ibid., p. 381.
[32]   For an extended analysis, see Bradley Quinn, *The Fashion of Architecture* (London: Berg Publishers, 2003), pp. 19–21. This strategy has been repeated at other stores like Dior in Omotesando.

Thus, with clothing as a means of socializing through the definition of individual and collective images, the contemporary idea of *building as cloth* represents a public tool of social inclusion that, in the case of retails, would be completed by means of consumerism. Seductive carnivalesque scenarios appeal to outright participation in the ritual of consumer culture that, according to Harald Gruendl, takes on Dionysian connotations.[33] An extreme example of this is represented by seasonal disguises of luxury stores through decorations of their exterior that play with the ornamental and ephemeral in a sort of celebration of these fashion paradigms. In 2007, the Matsuya Department Store in Ginza was temporally dressed up as the emblematic Louis Vuitton suitcase thanks to a projection of the *monogram multicolored print* that Takashi Murakami had designed for the label. The same artist, whose collaborations for Vuitton have been a prolific development of co-branding, has featured other iconic products through temporal exterior decorations for the brand's flagship stores in Omotesando, Tokyo, and New York (→**8**).

Final Observations: The Other Side of the Mirror

Within this context, architecture can be a tool equally able to articulate challenges and criticism addressed to some of the imperatives of neoliberal competitive production and transformative consumption. Concept shops, like Comme des Garçons Pocket stores, Dover Street Market in London and Ginza, or Maison Martin Margiela's boutiques, have based their commercial settlement on a sort of policy of discretion and even urban *invisibility* (→**9**). Some of these spaces mix several functions (art galleries, restaurants, even spaces for selling garden articles, etc.), provoking the essential feeling of taking part in a fashionable lifestyle that goes beyond the limits of the image.

Equally, since 2004, the founder of Comme des Garçons, fashion designer Rei Kawakubo, has defended a type of retailing called the *Guerrilla Stores*, which have been popping up in cities like Berlin, Stockholm, and Singapore, defying the rules of conventional brand competitiveness and the colonialism of great multinational companies. With *Guerrillazine: Extracts of a Corporate Nightmare*, she has fixed five instructions of this "urban commercial guerrilla": their transient presence in the urban space (not more than one year), the avoidance of commercial areas for the location, interior decoration that corresponds to the existing space, brand support of the partners that rent the local space, and a reasonable merchandise selection conformed

[33]   Harald Gruendl, EOOS, *The Death of Fashion: The Passage Rite of Fashion in the Show Window* (Vienna and New York: Springer, 2007), pp. 14–9.

(9) Comme des Garçons Store, Rue du Faubourg Saint-Honoré, Paris, interior design by Jean-Christophe Poggioli and Pierre Beucler (Architecture & associés) (Photo: Ana Llorente)

by garments from different seasons.[34] It is a proper initiative of democratization, both of high-end fashion and retail activities of the label itself. It reflects a positive depiction of the brand's mobility in atypical locations that avoids a hard investment in landmark/signature buildings, thus defying within this terrain (and for the sake of commercial development) the essence of architecture as "an omnipotent entity that actually fully satisfies a few."[35]

On the other hand, the dialogues between fashion and architecture are generating an emergent displacement of the latter to that sector, even configuring its active involvement in the industry from the basis of education, as is being demonstrated through academic programs like AA Visiting School Paris, directed by Jorge Ayala. Nevertheless, these intersections are also leading to networks focused on the development of architectural solutions for global issues related to political, economic, and environmental concerns. Fashion has been a source of research for interdisciplinary projects conceived by architects and professors like Toshiko Mori, who has counted on the experience of Dai Fujiwara for her academic programs at the Harvard Graduate School of Design. The circular weaving digital method that the textile engineer invented for fashion designer Issey Miyake has been presented as a prototype of a technology capable of providing low-cost solutions for architectural design and building.

[34]   See John Waters, *Role Models* (New York: Farrar, Straus and Giroux, 2010), pp. 128–32.

[35]   Translated from the Spanish: "una entidad omnipotente que, en realidad, satisface plenamente a unos pocos." David Moriente, *Poéticas arquitectónicas en el arte contemporáneo* (Madrid: Cátedra, 2011), p. 400.

(10) Paco Rabanne, *Unwearable dress*, Vogue UK, April 15, 1966 (Photo: David Montgomery)

Finally, fashion is constructing a means of redemption for architecture as a critical device by the (re)inscription of its industry on the board of creative and cultural reflection. The "architectural way of thinking" in clothing design has led to the possibility of the abstraction of the garment as a fashion object and the consequent (re)configuration of its perception and meanings. In this line, Paco Rabanne and his collection manifesto "12 Unwearable Dresses in Contemporary Materials" established, in the mid-sixties, the precedents of a sort of dystopian vision around the values of fulfillment promised by *ready-to-wear* system and the self-creative ethos. Alluding to architectural artifacts, and through the subversion of materials, Rabanne pushed the limits of the fashionable garment as portable clothing able to forge social and cultural identities (→**10**). Contemporary avant-garde designers still create pieces impossible to wear and consume, often referring to the impossible balance between rapid cycles of fashion and the needs that must be fulfilled by clothing design. One of the most impressive hybrid works is represented by the iconic wedding dress created by Yamamoto (Autumn/Winter 1998/1999), with an out-of-proportion hat and crinoline that turned out to be the metamorphosis of a tent (→**11**). Twelve years later, this creation has been transformed by the Wapping Project into a sort of inverted dome suspended from the

(11) Yohji Yamamoto, Oversized white silk wedding dress with bamboo crinoline and oversized hat supported by bamboo sticks, Autumn/Winter 1998 (Photo: Stephen Lock)

(12) *Yohji Making Waves,* Exhibition at the Wapping Project, London, March–July, 2011 Source: http://www.flickr.com/photos/kaz_pics/5821277810/sizes/z/in/photostream/

ceiling of the old Boiler House of the Wapping Hydraulic Power Station in London. The space was flooded in order to produce an unstable image of the straightened dress by its reflection on the water (→**12**), provoking a metaphor of the ephemeral and the unreachable essence of fashion's images.

Olaf Pfeifer

WHITE AS THE COLOR OF NEOLIBERALISM

When John Ruskin, in 1851, wrote his famous essay "On the Nature of Gothic," he devoted it to explaining what "proper" neo-Gothic architecture should and does look like.[1] Because Ruskin's analysis was overshadowed by the Industrial Revolution, mechanical reproduction, and its consequences for craftsmanship—and was thus all but impartial—he came up with a theory that linked the characters of an architectural style to certain essential characters of its builders: "savageness, love of change and nature, disturbed imagination, obstinacy, and generosity." These were the traits without which, asserted Ruskin, no true Gothic Style was possible, be there pointed arcs, tracery, gabled roofs, or not.

Our attempt today—as implied by the question titling this book— to describe the architecture of neoliberalism seems more difficult to me. Whereas Ruskin had the romanticized ideal of the free, medieval northern craftsmen, to whom he attributed the Gothic style, we have an obscure mixture of multinational, migrating, and oscillating consumers, developers, designers, and workforce; supposedly free, yet enslaved by their very own acts of consumption, their desires and needs. The idea that the workers of today, or even the architects, have a substantial influence on the *architectural style of neoliberalism* seems, realistically spoken, far-fetched.

[1]   John Ruskin, *The Stones of Venice* (1886; repr., New York: Cosimo Classics, 2010), p. 154.

Of course, if *neoliberal architecture* is defined as the architectural production of the age of neoliberalism, which, according to David Harvey, began roughly 1978,[2] there should be something to analyze. Since cathedrals are no longer en vogue, one might arguably decide for airports, train stations, and other transitory buildings to be the essential typology for the age of globalization—and end up with a description like the sufficiently known ones, given by Rem Koolhaas in his famous text "Junkspace"[3] or by Marc Augé in his book *Non-Places*.[4]

Instead, I would like to limit my theory-building to a single aspect of architecture and take a phenomenological approach to querying its significance, context, and possible meanings: the usage of the color *white*. White, as a color in Western architecture, has had a certain role (at least) since the beginning of classicism, where it marked the historical and cultural distance between classical antiquity and its representation as a remote yet ideal paradigm for society and architecture. In 1764, the founder of German archaeological science, Johann Joachim Winckelmann, wrote in his canonical publication on the subject, *Geschichte der Kunst des Alterthums*: "Since white is the color that reflects the most rays of light, and thus is most easily perceived, a beautiful body will be all the more beautiful the whiter it is."[5] Apparently even Winckelmann knew about traces of color on antique works of art, yet he dismissed the custom of painting marble and stone as a "barbarian exception." According to archaeologist Vinzenz Brinkmann, his followers kept up this stance for a long time, even though more and more evidence of color was found. One of Winckelmann's most influential followers and a major protagonist of the classicist project in the arts, Johann Wolfgang von Goethe, was well aware of the problems of representing classical antiquity as a guideline for modern society, and he was also aware of the fact that most of what his age (and ours) saw in antiquity was probably a projection—yet a very welcome one. "Only from afar, only separated from all that is common, only as bygone shall antiquity appear to us."[6]

[2]   David Harvey, *A Brief History of Neoliberalism* (Oxford: Oxford University Press, 2007), p. 1.
[3]   Rem Koolhaas, "Junkspace," ed. Jeremy Gilbert-Rolfe et al., *October* 100 (Spring 2002), pp. 175–90.
[4]   Marc Augé, *Non-Places: Introduction to an Anthropology of Supermodernity* (London et al.: Verso, 1995).
[5]   Johann Joachim Winckelmann, *History of the Art of Antiquity*, translation by Harry Francis Mallgrave (Los Angeles: Getty Publications, 2006), p. 195.
[6]   My translation of "Nur aus der Ferne, nur von allem Gemeinen getrennt, nur als vergangen muß das Altertum uns erscheinen" from Johann Wolfgang von Goethe, "Winckelmann und sein Jahrhundert," in *Hamburger Ausgabe*, vol. 12 (München: C.H. Beck, 2008), p. 109; compare also: Jürgen Jacobs, "Athen in Weimar: Zu Goethes und Winckelmanns Klassizismus," in *Dass gepfleget werde der feste Buchstab*, ed. Lothar Bluhm (Trier: WVT Wissenschaftlicher Verlag Trier, 2001), p. 109.

My conclusion is that Goethe and Winckelmann's era already used the white representation of antiquity within classicist art and architecture as an instrument to clearly mark the distance between now and then, between abstract idealization and naïve repetition. However, the built images of classicist *reconstructions* seem to have been stronger than the scientific debate, since even today we call a certain tone of white *antique white* and not *classicist white*, which would be more appropriate.

An example of modern architecture that uses white in a way similar to the approach taken by the classicists is Eero Saarinen's TWA Terminal at New York's John F. Kennedy Airport. The building, because of its organic and undulating form, is often depreciated as a flat-out bird analogy. "Forget the bird", however, was, critic Edgar Kaufmann's verdict, pointing to the "magnificence which belongs to the average man." [7] In fact, for the air travelers of the nineteen-sixties, the terminal represented a highly ceremonial—that is, ritualistic—space. Sweeping stairs, wide oval doors, and a grand roof and gallery make for the staging of perfect farewells. One especially interesting feature is the sloping walkway that connects terminal and satellite (→**1**). The upwardly bent tube with its indirectly lit walls makes departing travelers literally fade into the white backlight as they transcend its crest. Because of the lack of any detail inside the tunnel and the unreal lighting, distance is hard to estimate, which turns the simple enterprise of boarding a plane into a dramatic experience that seems like an expedition into an unclear, distant future.

One may, like Winckelmann, argue that white is the color best suited for sculpture and the sculptural, since it allows for the greatest contrast and depth of shadow; but then again, it excludes any trace of materiality (other than marble) and haptic qualities, which are certainly important for many types of sculpture, especially non-representational or non-illusionistic types of sculpture, such as buildings—let alone the traces of origin, aging, and authorship that are virtually excluded by the universal purity of whiteness. This is, however, precisely the reason to use white: it represents *non-information,* suppressing certain aspects in order to push others to the foreground. It acts as a whiteout.

The white reproduction and reconstruction of antique sculpture and buildings, even if conducted against better knowledge, serves to indicate a level of abstraction and ephemeral estrangement from daily life and coincides with the Christian topic of *divine light* and *purity.* Central to Christian mythology is the idea that humans, just as nature, were created as perfection before being rendered imperfect sinners through interaction with society; they can, however become more

---

[7]   Edgar Kaufmann, "Inside Eero Saarinen's TWA Building," *Interiors* 121, no. 12 (July 1962), p. 87.

(1) Departing passengers literally fade into white. Eero Saarinen, Trans World Flight Center, 1962, John F. Kennedy Airport, New York City
© Sherrie Allan, sallanscorner. wordpress.com

perfect and closer to God by abiding religious rules and purging the desire to commit sins, thus once again approximating the state of perfect purity. It is easy to understand why white is used as a symbol for purity: it will be stained by any other color and it cannot be mixed from other pigments aside from white ones (except by chemical reaction). Yet it will not change the hue of any other color and is itself the perfect background—representing the pure, immaculate state that everything was created in. The idea of Immaculate Conception, as well as the white wedding dress as a representation of the bride's innocence, illustrates this very well.

Ethnologist Mary Douglas has explained the cultural reasons and needs for purification rituals, specifically in her famous book *Purity and Danger*. She points out that the idea of purity denotes the existence of an order, along which anything can be declared more or less clean. Dirt is not absolute but relative to a context: soil is not recognized as dirty unless it is carried inside a house; shoes are not necessarily dirty in and of themselves, but on the dining table they are dirty; not even microorganisms can be seen as pollution unless they have spilled over into the wrong habitat. "Dirt [is] matter out of place," concludes Douglas.[8] So the fact that disorder cannot be perceived as such without the existence of an underlying system of order— "Where there is dirt, there is system"[9]—led her to the conclusion that many rituals of purification simply exist to point to the existence and strength of that order, thereby actually establishing it, as well as to commemorate the fact that there is a certain danger associated with breaking the given rule.

[8]   Mary Douglas, *Purity and Danger: An Analysis of Concepts of Pollution and Taboo* (London et al.: Routledge, 2007), p. 36.
[9]   Ibid.

(2) Typical box pews inside of a Puritan church in Millville, Massachusetts, 1769
© The Chestnut Street Meeting House and Cemetery Association

Purification rituals are central (not only) to Christian religion, and many major related developments have started as an attempt to purify its rules. One of these movements was, as the name already suggests, the *Puritan* Church. The Puritans originally were an offspring of the Anglican Church influenced by Calvinism, who dissented on the point of infant baptism and church membership by birth; to them, religion was the result of a personal experience and thus could not be governed by the state. Puritans were important during the English Revolution under Oliver Cromwell (where they acted as iconoclasts) but quickly lost their influence because of the congregational nature of their beliefs. Many Puritans emigrated to the Netherlands and to the American colonies in the following centuries, where Puritanism, and its Congregationalist offspring (like the Baptists denomination), became one of the main religious streams of the United States. Puritanism is *defined* by the abolition or even prohibition of many other Christian rituals and symbols—such as Christmas, dancing, the holy cross, depictions of God, saints, and the Holy Spirit (not even as a dove) inside of churches—as well as by a number of rules and rituals to replace the abolished ones, whereby each member actively expresses his or her belief and allegiance to the congregation, such as adult baptism by immersion. Puritans were not supposed to waste any time that could be used sensibly—that is, for work—and they thus often came to considerable wealth quickly, which was not against their beliefs; however, they were also not supposed to show their wealth by spending. Critics of Puritan heritage have even gone so far as to say that "Puritanism [is] the haunting fear that someone, somewhere, may be happy."[10] Like many religions, evangelicals have certain ideas

[10]   Henry L. Mencken, *A Book of Burlesques* (New York: Alfred A. Knopf, 1916).

about marriage and sexual life. Many of the smaller congregations were focused on charismatic leaders—nowadays, we would call them a *cult*—who oftentimes were pretty experimental about the rules that they prescribed for their community, sometimes making wild turns from celibacy to polygamy, but in most cases there were rules about sexual life. Adjustment to these rules could be interpreted as a reaction to the lack of new members, but also as early and experimental forms of biopolitical rule, to use Foucault's term, an essential technique of governance within the neoliberal *empire*.

Max Weber, in his book *Protestant Ethics and the Spirit of Capitalism*,[11] described ascetic Protestantism, central to Puritan belief, as a basis of capitalist development: the combination of Puritan work ethos and the prohibition to waste money on obvious luxury led to the accumulation of capital, which, in turn, needed to be spent for productive enterprises instead of luxuries.

Early Puritan churches (→**2**) were mostly pure in the sense of simplicity. They were not necessarily all white—for paint was a luxury as well—but rather ascetic, and they definitely were not embellished with murals or painted ceilings. The altar was a simple, wooden desk, and most of the seats were built as *box pews* by the families who paid for owning them. These boxes can be interpreted not only as an early model for typically American fundraising, but also as a visible symbol for the order of Congregationalist belief and the level of social control. A family's social status would be expressed by the position of their box pew inside the church: the pews up front were more expensive and hard to come by, even for newcomers with money to spend, which accurately implemented both a seniority principle *and* a monetary one. It is known that a family's social status would improve upon moving further up toward the front of the church.

The example shown here (→**3**) is by Robert Mills of South Carolina, who also built the Washington Monument. Mills was a contemporary of James Hoban, the architect of the White House. The church shown here was also clearly influenced by revolutionary architecture—as the omission of a central axis shows—and also by classicism. Many of the later Puritan, Congregationalist, and Baptist church buildings show strong classical influence, and it is also said that Puritan thought was "full of classicisms."[12]

[11]   Max Weber, *The Protestant Ethics and the Spirit of Capitalism* (London: Fitzroy Dearborn, 2001).
[12]   Since this church is located in Camden, South Carolina, it probably was not built as a Puritan one, for the Puritan influence in the beginning was mainly in New England, and only after the "Great Awakening" did it extended across the land.

Another aspect of Puritan ideology, the "Enfield Sermon,"[13] shows another principle of governance. It established the idea that God, at any arbitrary moment in time, may punish an individual, even if they were abiding the rules at that particular moment; and that a sin may not only be punished on the spot, but also later. This put the believers in a constant state of fear—which, as a governing principle, remains very deeply rooted in the United States of today.

[13]   The legendary "Enfield Sermon" (1741) by the Puritan preacher Jonathan Edwards was part of the *Great Awakening*, which was a mass reevangelization of large parts of rather secular population groups by various traveling preachers. In order to become a mass-compatible religion, Puritanism had to *soften* in certain ways, but it also became—as opposed to its originally congregational nature—a tool of governance.

To summarize, among the Puritans and similar religious streams, purity and the related rituals serve as an ordering principle to establish a social order within the community. White may serve, on the one hand, as a symbol of purity and, on the other, as a symbol for an order based on the absence of sin (as in purism) and on the unreachable distance of an abstract ideal (as in classicism).

White is the color of both abstraction and projection. At the same time, white surfaces require—and signify—high levels of maintenance, often ritualistic in nature (such as the periodic whitewashing of plain houses), and control (usually prevention of [ab]use by those unauthorized or excluded).

Iconoclasm

In a section of their book *Multitude,* Michael Hardt and Antonio Negri argue that after the year 726, during the reign of Emperor Leon III, when icons were forbidden and had to be destroyed, this iconoclasm became part of the power structure of the Byzantine Empire.[14] The absence of imagery in churches was, according to Hardt and Negri, supposed to prevent any *direct* contact between the people and their religious longings, but to have those religious needs be dependent and concentrated on the clergy and thus on the state. If this argument is valid, and we assume that image consumption is a need for today's information junkies, it means that the absence of images in any space must have a similar effect as the suppression of sexual desires and religious images within religious communities, such as, for instance, in the case of the Puritans. Thus, *white*, or the absence of images, becomes a symbol for the presence of an *invisible* system of order; it could even symbolize the replacement of a visible system of order with an invisible, internalized one. This could help to explain the fetishization of whiteness in certain work and leisure environments—they function as modern monasteries. For example, in advertisements for the wellness industry, white is used as a symbol for ritualistic purification but also as a pointer to the (omni)presence of a powerful yet invisible system of order, based on a willfully imposed ritual governed by the subject itself (!), which fosters calmness within the rushed world of information overload.

In Christian semiology, white—as the absence of objects and images—thus always points to the existence of an invisible, powerful, and internalized system of order; a metaphor for the omnipresence of God and the Holy Spirit, as well as for the exclusiveness of deity in Semitic religions.

[14]   Michael Hardt and Antonio Negri, *Multitude: War and Democracy in the Age of Empire* (New York et al.: Penguin, 2005) p. 324 ff.

An almost parallel metaphor from film architecture is Stanley Kubrick's *2001: A Space Odyssey*. The interior of the space station (→**4**) displays a perfect, sublime white design, which contrasts with most of the shown humans, who wear regular, old-fashioned-looking uniforms and suits. The white here obviously symbolizes the perfection and divine omnipresence of the super computer HAL, and his intentions that are noble by definition.

Since my aim here is to disclose the symbolic values of whiteness within neoliberalism, I shall now analyze some examples from the period that we commonly call neoliberal, that is, since the nineteeneighties. One major goal of the neoliberal doctrine is to shift power away from nation-states to markets; and the incarnation of the market is the city. Creating images for cities and marketing them—partly also in order to constitute their independence from government subsidies—has been a major project of cultural politics. Since neoliberalism and its protagonists do not necessarily share religious zeal with early Puritanism, the mechanics of controlling their desires focus on consumption and culture.[15] Nowadays, protagonists of economic liberalism show an unquenchable thirst for cultural self-affirmation, which has replaced religious zeal; hence the building of cultural institutions, such as museums, is as important in the age of neoliberalism as the building of churches and monasteries was in late medieval times. Even today, any Asian city that wishes to become visible as a market at first implements a set of cultural institutions, and there

[15]   This is a reception of Foucault, for whom liberalism, as well as neoliberalism, is a mode of government first of all, though one that pretends to work without much executive power; instead, the control is exerted by what Foucault calls "biopolitics." See Michel Foucault, *The Birth of Biopolitics: Lectures at the Collège de France 1978–1979* (Basingstoke and New York: Palgrave Macmillan, 2008).

(5) Reality or photomontage? Worry-free white interior at SANAA's Rolex Learning Center, Lausanne
© 2010 SANAA

is always a museum among these. Museums of contemporary art, which function as an anchor for the art market, are almost always of the *white cube* type.

As Brian O'Doherty has pointed out in his classic essay "Inside the White Cube," white—within the art world—also implicates the separation of object and context, replacing the picture frame; it is the color of the displacement of an art object. "A gallery is constructed along laws as rigorous as those for building a medieval church. The outside world must not come in, so windows are usually sealed off. Walls are painted white. The ceiling becomes the source of light."[16]

O'Doherty also notes that this "gives the space a presence possessed by other spaces where conventions are preserved through the repetition of a closed system of values. Some of the sanctity of the church, the formality of the courtroom, the mystique of the experimental laboratory joins with chic design to produce a unique chamber of esthetics. So powerful are the perceptual fields of force within this chamber that once outside it, art can lapse into secular status. Conversely, things become art in a space where powerful ideas about art focus on them."[17] The white cube isolates the work of art from both context and time. Similarly, where architects work with historic building substance, white generally functions as the layer of separation between objects and background (or canvas, if you will).[18] If a work of art can be constituted by giving it a white background, it also will be mobilized this way—the global exchange and trade of art would not be possible without the unifying omnipresence of the white cube.

[16]   Brian O'Doherty, *Inside the White Cube: The Ideology of the Gallery Space*, expanded edition (Berkeley and Los Angeles: University of California Press, 1999), p. 15.
[17]   Ibid., p. 14.
[18]   I am thinking of the work of Carlo Scarpa, for example, at the Castelvecchio in Verona, and many of those influenced by Scarpa.

(6) Jürgen Meyer H., installation
for Calvin Klein, 2009
(Photo: Ludger Paffrath)

(7) Vanessa Beecroft, *VB 35*, 1998,
performance at Solomon R.
Guggenheim Museum, New York
(Photo: Mario Sorrenti)
© Vanessa Beecroft

Removing objects and subjects alike from their respective contexts and making them available to global markets and different interpretations is essentially the nature of globalization, as well as of neoliberalism. Pascal Gielen, quoting Elena Filipovich in his collection of essays titled *The Murmuring of the Artistic Multitude*, has elaborated on the question as to what makes the white cube so appealing, even to divergent ideological worlds: "The answer is somewhat predictable: 'order,' 'rationality,' 'universality' and '(Western) modernity.' Two other ascribed qualities, however, deserve particular attention within this narrative, namely 'neutrality' and (especially) 'disconnection from the context.' The white cube cherished by biennales and curators thus cuts itself off from the variable environment in which it finds itself."[19] Gielen goes on to say that "the white cube is so widespread as a global institution because its staging of autonomy denies any political, economic or religious entanglement. The integration of these spheres in the museum also threatens to neutralize any problem or social conflict within the safe zone of fiction. Perhaps that is what makes the white cube so beloved, and very exceptionally even by totalitarian regimes. Within an all-encompassing neo-liberalism, the ideological silence of the white space is a godsend."[20]

Actually, these principles of universal white as the color of isolation not only work for art, but for humans as well: the way to turn humans into a global workforce is to equalize their desires and needs, and consumerism is one of the tools for this. White has a certain role in consumerism.

Advertisement and Commodification

In advertisement, white is the background color that suggests lightness, simplicity and ease of use, purity, truth, and freedom—or at least no obligations. Electronic devices, for example, tend to be white if the corporate identity of the manufacturer claims simplicity, and black if the aim is to look powerful. The *black box* is a mystery, while the white one promises light(hearted)ness, joy, and fun.

One of the reasons for this is of course decontextualization. A white background is actually the absence of background and context. It is also a metaphor for the absence of problems, difficulties, complexities, worries, et cetera.

Photographers have developed a special yet simple technique to isolate an object from its background, called high-key photography. Technically, a black background works just as well to isolate an object; but

[19]   Pascal Gielen, "The Biennale: A Post-Institution for Immaterial Labour," *The Murmuring of the Artistic Multitude: Global Art, Memory and Post-Fordism* (Amsterdam: Valiz, 2010), p. 40.
[20]   Ibid., p. 41.

the lack of clarity about what may be in the dark areas adds a momentum of fear or hesitation.

Anything or anybody presented on white becomes an image of a commodity, aestheticizing its details like under a magnifying glass, and renders it readily available to our access, thus turning the subject into an object, even if a person is depicted. This works particularly well if we show only part of a person or object. This is because our brain completes the missing parts, thereby actively imagining the situation, which is an act of projecting our own desires onto the object shown, thus making it our own and reflecting our own narcissism. This process is referred to as *fetishization*.

There are many examples of architectural renderings that try to look like commercial advertisements (→**5**). One may argue that this is partly due to the collage technique and the source material that is used to edit details like people into the abstract renderings, but if the finished building looks just like a collage of people on a white background as well, I find this a bit disconcerting. However, in the case of the Japan-based architectural firm SANAA, it even correlates with the motto "People Meet in Architecture," which they used for their 2010 Venice Biennale curatorship. Coincidence, synesthetic work of art, or com-modification strategy?

By contrast, showing a much older and more heavy-handed yet equal-ly white example of neoliberal strategies of conversion and gentrifica-tion is the Grande Arche de la Défense. In fact, despite its monumen-tal style and positioning, this structure is pretending to be a stage for human interaction, and specifically for that reason it has an internal, tensile architecture to give humans a slight chance to inhibit such a giant wind channel.

My last architectural example is the work of Jürgen Meyer H. and his office, a shooting star of Berlin's architectural and creative scene. A short look at their homepage shows Meyer's interest in form—or should I say *shape*, to use the dichotomy established by Robert Somol to differentiate between content/context-driven critical and "cool" (if not to say decorative) architecture.[21] Obviously, not everything is white, but almost everything shows an interest in sculptural, expres-sive lines that almost frame the building volume like an exoskeleton or a car chassis, which nevertheless and curiously seems to relate to the building like an interchangeable click-on shell to a mobile phone. Meyer recently also designed a showroom with a white stage for Calvin Klein (→**6**). It is probably not only me who feels the proximity

[21]   In Somol's case, the apprehensive description of the Office of Met-ropolitan Architecture's new line of products: Robert E. Somol, "12 Reasons to Get Back in Shape," in *Content: Triumph of Realization; Rem Koolhaas*, ed. Rem Koolhaas (Cologne: Taschen, 2004), pp. 86–7.

to the art installations of Vanessa Beecroft here. Beecroft's work (→**7**), typically showing a large number of naked or almost-naked women standing inside a white-cube-type cultural institution or gallery and confronting the visitors, is highly ambivalent and subject to either ab-solute love or condemnation of her critics: on one hand, Beecroft's installation photographs sell very well, probably also because the col-lector gains an excuse to own a giant pinup. Beecroft's work sells out on the female body: her models have shaved body hair and wear high heels, body makeup, and sometimes even wigs. They are trans-formed into objects—either sex objects or art objects, in any case, fetishes—and are subject to normative preselection (only recently has Beecroft included non-white models), and they certainly help to promote a certain female body image. Yet all of this can be seen as a criticism of exactly those strategies, even if Beecroft typically re-mains very ambivalent in interpreting her own work. More recently, Beecroft's work is more often read as a commentary on the position of the individual in today's precarious relations of self-marketing and work relations, which never stop to include the whole personality and body. I am very inclined to interpret Jürgen Meyer H.'s Calvin Klein advertisement in a similar way; yet he takes the step from a cultural institution to a private *sponsor*—a client.

Let me conclude—and offer an answer to the question posed in the title of this book—with Brian O'Doherty's closing words from *Inside the White Cube*, which is a resigned commentary on the fact that, once more, in the eighties (at the onset of neoliberalism) art had been co-opted by commerce:

"The new work's [only] defense against smooth consumption is in its various masks, in which complex internal ironies are decipherable."[22]

[22]   O'Doherty, *Inside the White Cube*, p. 113. Insertion by the author.

Oliver Ziegenhardt

BAUKULTURINDUSTRIE—A POLEMIC

Clever enough, the title of this publication doesn't state "there is" but asks "is there" architecture that could be labeled "neoliberal." Adding a political category—or one of political economy—to architecture is always problematic. In answering the question as to whether there was *socialist architecture*, it is not legal to put Stalinist megalomania, the white cubes of the Bauhaus modernists—most of them leftists or even communists—the pseudo-capitalist high-rises in China, and the philistrous *Hausbau* construction in the former German Democratic Republic into the same pot, together with the community buildings of Red Vienna. All of them were built under (quasi) socialist regimes, but to immediately label their architecture *socialist* would suggest that there are political features inscribed into form. It is most doubtable that there is a formal uttering that makes an architecture *fascist* or *communist*, *capitalist* or *socialist*, *conservative* or *liberal*. It is most naïve to think glass automatically expresses democracy, whereas a thick wall of stone stands for repressive systems. Hence, there can be no talk about *the* neoliberal architecture (at least as far as architecture is conceived in terms of form). The text at hand is an effort to prove this thesis.

In questioning what the architectural equivalent of neoliberalism would be, isn't the first thing that comes to mind the CI architecture of transnational companies? That of great financial institutes? The pseudo-avant-garde of second generation blobmasters who claim *parametricism* was the New International Style? Vast malls and shopping centers which demonstrate that shopping is the most important cultural expression of today? Would it be architecture not affordable for underdogs but only for global(ized) elites?

Superficially, one might say that *neoliberal architecture* is the one that results from globalization, that is, market friendly and easy to identify. However, what I shall try to show here is that the debate must take place at a different level, empowered by the recourse of political science. This article seeks to contribute to a renewed discourse about architecture and politics.

Architecture as a Political Act

The common discussions about architecture as art—as the production of space, as the material representation of social space, as the container of atmosphere, as the major principle of order in the arts, as technical engineering plus decoration, or (most prominently among contemporary architects) as design of images and surfaces—all neglect that architecture (not first of all, but to a large extent) is a political act. It is undisputedly always an act of mediation and confrontation. The decision of building, the decision of designing, even the decision of drawing the first line is a political act. The further you come in designing or even building, the more involved in politics you get. When you are designing a single-family house, it is a contribution to the debate of how the sprawl is the result of too many single-family houses, not mentioning that even here there is certain politic interaction between the members of the family. The larger your project gets, the more you turn from designer to politician, playing the role of mediator between the most different groups of people.

Hence, architectural theory—if understood as the theory of circumstances in the production of architecture—must turn toward political theory when facing a political question like the relation to neoliberalism. Architecture and politics are both instruments of organizing and structuring society, so it is legal to assume a close relation. In other words: if architecture represents a device for the organization of social life, architectural theory is likewise a vehicle for the exploration and explanation of living environments, and hence has always been a political and social theory of community.

In the following, a particular aspect of the relation of architecture and politics will be presented. It is not about political architecture, nor does it concern the architecture in which political action takes place, such as parliaments, embassies, party headquarters, and so on, nor the architecture of the great financial companies or the corporate design of global players. These are the major topics in the general discourse of architecture and politics, which in my opinion neglect a certain side aspect that must be mentioned. It is the aspect of *architectural politics*, shifting the focus away from buildings and rather toward institutions and networks, where discourse is produced and conducted by a mixture of architects, theorists, critics (maybe post-critics), and other figures beyond the realm of *building*—like representatives of the building industry, the chambers of architects and sibling organizations, architectural magazines and newsletters, units for architectural education, like many departments for architectural theory and history. Architectural politics is more than a special branch of national culture politics dealing with design and architectural tasks, and much more than a special branch of infrastructure dealing with built environment. Nowadays, it is first and foremost the marketing of the profession *architect* and the marketing of ideas that arise in the realm of architectural discourse. In other words, architectural politics functions more and more as a market for architectural *products*.

The economization of architectural politics goes hand in hand with the depolitization of architectural discourse. Architectural theory has great historical affinities toward art, philosophy, technology, and politics, but the last one is currently considerably underrated, especially concerning the criticism of ideology. Because architecture is the most public form of *Gestaltung*, or design, it is and has always been a target of ideology. Ideology is the messaging and targeting form of certain thinking, whether it originates from philosophy, economy, or elsewhere. The ideology predominant today is so-called *neoliberalism*.

The Concept of *Vitalpolitik*

The neoliberal project has its origins in economic theories, but has grown into all areas of everyday life. Topoi basic to neoliberalism, like the demolition of the welfare state and the expansion of the markets, contribute massively to an economization of everyday life, including the production of architecture. As Keith Dixon and Mario Candeias have shown, neoliberalism is a so-called neo-corporatist model, gaining hegemony by incorporating all three sections of society: state, market, and civil society.[1] They have shown that, after the first generation of neoliberal politics like Reaganomics or Thatcherism, we now face the absurd fact that the reconstitution of neoliberalism in Europe was made possible by social democratic politicians like Gerhard Schroeder and Tony Blair.[2] The meaning of the term neoliberalism has shifted from basic market radicality to an all-embracing system producing consensus and accepting a lack of alternatives.

In this case, it does not matter whether building management and design methods are of interest, but whether they encourage the in-

[1]   Mario Candeias, "High-Tech, Hartz und Hegemonie," http://www2.
       bdwi.de/uploads/mario_candeias_high-tech_hartz_und_hegemonie.pdf
       (accessed June 2012).
[2]   Keith Dixon, *Ein würdiger Erbe: Anthony Blair und der Thatcherismus*
       (Konstanz: Universitätsverlag Konstanz, 2000), pp. 62–3.

stitutionalization, normativization, and marketing of culture related to an increasing de-democratization. The critique of this ideology must entail a skeptical attitude toward normative *good taste* and lead to criticism of an *expertocracy* judgment of "good architecture." However, before we engage in this critical endeavor, it is necessary to take a closer look at the neoliberal project.

When we discuss the implementation of neoliberalism on a larger scale, the political systems of *Reaganomics* in the United States and *Thatcherism* in the United Kingdom soon come to mind—where the hammer hit hardest in smashing the welfare state, weakening the unions, and pushing forward the privatization of former state property and state tasks, which are outsourced to private companies. But although the implementation of neoliberalism—not mentioning the example of Chile—was done by right-wing figures like Reagan and Thatcher, it was most popularized and drawn into the mainstream by social democrats: it was the famous "Schroeder-Blair" paper of 1999[3] in which the cutting of the social state, the welfare state, was finally brought to the top of the political agenda, as were strategies of assertion. The results and consequences are well known, in Germany the Agenda 2010 and the Hartz IV welfare laws, for example.

To understand the story behind this, we must take a look into the history of neoliberalism, where we will find that there are several *neoliberalisms*. For instance, the so-called *ordoliberalism* as a special German form of neoliberalism. Ordoliberalism was the political economy framing the *Soziale Marktwirtschaft*, or the social market economy. This theory of a rather strong but not interfering state that controls market forces gave rise to the famous *Wirtschaftswunder*, or economic miracle. Wilhelm Röpke, Alfred Müller-Armack, Ludwig Ehrhardt, and—most interesting in our context—Alexander Rüstow are key figures in the social market economy, originally an ordoliberal idea, as published in the magazine ORDO, the herald of the ordoliberals. In some of his countless articles, Rüstow coined the term *Vitalpolitik*, or vital politics. In contrast to the Foucauldian term *biopolitics*—which just like neoliberalism is used only in a pejorative sense, and no one would ever label himself as having an affinity toward biopolitics or even opting for it—Rüstow invented the concept of Vitalpolitik in a fully positive sense, pushing it forward as the only alternative to *Sozialpolitik*, or social politics, which was unbearable for neoliberalists.

Of course Rüstow, Röpke, and the others were members of the famous Mont Pelerin Society, which is the foundation myth of neoliberalism. In 1938, there was a conference taking place in Paris, the Colloque Walter Lippmann, where politicians, philosophers, economists,

---

[3]   Mario Candeias, "From a fragmented left to mosaic," *Luxemburg* 2 (2009), p. 5.

and others met to invent new strategies for saving liberalism, or for the sake of a renewed liberalism and its forms of implementation. At this conference, the group decided to form a think tank which was to develop concepts for a new liberalism and set up a series of future conferences to establish continuity in meeting and working. In 1942, the Mont Pelerin Society was founded in Switzerland, atop a mountain near Geneva called Mont Pelerin, meaning pilgrim mountain.[4] In 1954, Alexander Rüstow introduced his concept of Vitalpolitik that was intended to replace the Sozialpolitik of the leftist governments.[5] Friedrich Hayek, another early neoliberal, labeled the term *social* as a so-called *weasel word*, an expression as quick and agile as a weasel, showing up and vanishing the next second. Rüstow based his considerations on Hayek's explanation of the social and developed the counterexample of Vitalpolitik, which interferes strongly in the private life of the individual. Rüstow dreamed of a village-like society—which may sound somewhat philistine, but in a special way it was typical for German politics of that era—where everybody has a car or a motorcycle and where new villages are established all over the country. Thirty years later this came true, as you can see in the vast suburban landscapes. Not integration but pseudo-individualization was the aim of Vitalpolitik, treating everybody as a singularity and avoiding any form of collectivity. So, Vitalpolitik means an all-embracing system of interference of the state into everyone's business, leisure, and so on with an aim to improve the vital situation or, plainly stated, everyday life. Unlike most neoliberals, Rüstow rejected the idea of a weak state dominated by economists in favor of a corporatist system where all three sectors of society—state, market, civil society—would be interacting. Although Rüstow's concept of vital politics wasn't a huge success in his time, much more of it has survived subliminally in today's conditions.[6] The all-embracing system mentioned above focuses a lot on architecture, on housing, on the built environment of the individual, addressing not only experts but literally everyone who is concerned—or struck—by architecture. But how should the container look that shall comprise all that? And what would be the common name of these extensive applications of Vitalpolitik to the production of built environment?

---

[4]   The MPS still exists today and major figures of present neoliberalism are members, such as Jean Claude Trichet, the former chairman of the European Central Bank, or Josef Ackermann, the former head of Deutsche Bank.

[5]   See Alexander Ruestow, "Sozialpolitik oder Vitalpolitik?" *Mitteilungen der Industrie- und Handelskammer zu Dortmund* (Nov. 15, 1951), pp. 453–9.

[6]   Just recently, in November 2012, a conference was held in Darmstadt on the topic of *Vitalpolitik*. See http://www.eh-darmstadt.de/fileadmin/user_upload/PDFs/Aktuell/Tagungen/2012_Tagung_Vitalpolitik.pdf (accessed December 2012).

Baukultur as an Agent of Hegemony

Surely it is well known that there are some expressions originating from German language that have been carried over into other languages without being really translated, for instance *Zeitgeist*, *Aufklärung*, *Gemütlich*, *Gestaltung*, *Gestalt*, *Denkmal*, maybe *Wirtschaftswunder*. In recent years, the same could be said for the term *Baukultur*, or building culture. Numerous organizations, initiatives, and corporations are now dealing with Baukultur and moreover label themselves as the Agency for Baukultur, the Academy for Baukultur, and so on.[7] French and British magazines took over the term referring to a typically German relation between architecture and politics.[8] In recent years—no more than ten to fifteen—the term Baukultur has become ubiquitous. It carries with it a large backpack of different meanings. However, unlike the previously mentioned terms, which have both an everyday life meaning and also a scientific one, Baukultur has undergone only a few scientific considerations or reflections. There are very few attempts to establish a scientific discourse around it. The most elaborate attempt was undertaken by Eduard Führ, when he worked on the issue of his Internet magazine *Cloud Cuckoo Land 2* from the year 2003, following an eponymous conference. And furthermore, compared to the countless articles produced in order to implement and to promote Baukultur in a fully affirmative sense, critical voices are seldom heard. Nearly everyone seems to agree that we need to produce good Baukultur, that this is an aim for society as a whole ("Baukultur? Yes, please!"), that it is both desirable and necessary for the satisfying living environment, in other words, for the vital situation. Baukultur is more humble than the much noble *Baukunst*, which implies that a building is a work of art, not restricted by pragmatic requirements. Baukultur is considerably less bound to specific professionals, as architecture is to architects. And as opposed to *Bauwesen*, it comprises much more non-technical and non-industrial processes. Hence, the phenomenon Baukultur—which can be translated into English only superficially as building culture—must be understood in its genesis, potentials, and manifestations. And it must be made clear that this concept is quite susceptible to being occupied. It needs an agency, a promoter, may be even a solicitor—and it has found one.

[7]   See the Akademie für Baukultur of Peter Graf Pininski, the Rat für Baukultur, the forum StadtBauKultur, and so on.
[8]   Matthew Trigg, "Baukultur: The Term Everyone Should Know," http://urbantimes.co/2012/02/baukultur/ (accessed June 2012). "'Architecture' once filled much of the space, when it combined a wider range of activities and ideas than it does today. Unfortunately, the term has today been boxed in by the need for particular professionals to distinguish and protect themselves and their work. The average person has been largely excluded from the Vitruvian idea of architecture."

Around the year 2000, several centers for architectural politics and Baukultur—for the German-speaking countries—arose simultaneously in Europe as restorative counteractions against postmodernism's one-way-ticketed pluralism in order to establish a new *Leitkultur*, or guiding culture. The most famous and most important Baukultur organization in Germany is the Federal Foundation for Baukultur,[9] while in Austria it is the Austrian Platform for Architectural Policy and Building Culture,[10] cofounded by Volker Dienst in 2001 in Vienna. The Federal Foundation for Baukultur is a brainchild of the Chamber of Architects, the Ministry for Building and Housing, the building industry, and many others. Since its origination, the term Baukultur has spread widely among architects, engineers, and chamber bureaucrats, as well as real estate developers, who use the term much more than the erratic *architecture*, which is too neatly linked to one profession. The term Baukultur takes a hegemonic approach because it comprises nearly every branch of architecture and its production: from competition to the marketing of one's own profession, from the teaching of architecture in schools to awards, from nepotist cooperations to a wide range of networks of both scholars and creatives, from communication between architects and laypeople, between architects and commissioners, between architects and politicians. This has been forming a huge *Kulturindustrie*, or cultural industry, which can be called the *Baukulturindustrie*.[11] Great efforts are expended to reach cultural hegemony, with the production of many publications and flyers, the arranging of conferences and symposia, et cetera. In Germany, the Federal Foundation for Baukultur can be seen as a tool for hegemony.

Undisputedly, the term hegemony is a key word in the discourse on neoliberal theory or, more precisely, in its critique. Its meaning in political science derives from Antonio Gramsci, an Italian—or, more precisely, a Sardinian—unorthodox Marxist, who was in jail under the Mussolini regime. While incarcerated, he was still conceptualizing and writing political essays, which have been edited and freshly published in the last ten years, thus giving a good example of unorthodox Marxism that clearly defines the concept of hegemony in its cultural dominance and also the role of intellectuals in society in order to obtain this hegemony. Gramsci invented the concept of an "organic intellectual," which is a figure that uses his brains and his highly intellectual capacity in service of a certain ideology. Gramsci clearly

[9]   See http://www.bmvbs.de/EN/BuildingAndHousing/BuildingCulture/ FederalFoundationBaukultur/federal-foundation-for-baukultur_node.html (accessed July 2013).

[10]   See http://www.bmvbs.de/EN/BuildingAndHousing/BuildingCulture/ FederalFoundationBaukultur/federal-foundation-for-baukultur_node.html (accessed July 2013).

[11]   Of course, the term *Kulturindustrie* derives from Theodor W. Adorno and Max Horkheimer's book *Dialectic of Enlightment*, where it forms the central chapter, yet here another meaning is added.

differentiates cultural dominance in a totalitarian system of order and obedience from a hegemonic system that produces consensual ideas by means of seduction and persuasion. He states that the power and cultural dominance in a new capitalist society will not be achieved through violence and terror, but by slowly undermining discourse and establishing a new form of cultural arousal to promote an idea, which is why the organic intellectuals are needed. They are recruited not only by scientists and philosophers, but also by chairpeople and organizers of societal processes that are stimulating and assure a certain societal hegemony via state-run and/or ideological vehicles like education, media, political parties, and interest groupings. The organic intellectual differs from the classic intellectual; while the latter forms a proper class itself, the former is produced by any class of its own. The social group that strives for hegemony tries everything to assimilate the classic intellectuals while producing its own organic intellectuals. Organic intellectuals are not necessarily bound to science, but rather to any form of cultural language, of emotion and experience that cannot be uttered by broad masses.

For the phenomenon Baukultur and, more precisely, the Federal Foundation for Baukultur, there is a group of organic intellectuals who appear throughout the scene. Very important people—like Karl Ganser, Peter Conradi,[12] Werner Durth, and many others who contribute to the Baukulturindustrie—seek both to give advice to politicians and to market their own profession. Their aim besides the improvement of the quality of the built environment is to increase the number of publications on Baukultur in order to establish broad discourse in the whole of society; in fact, major figures of the Baukulturindustrie are driven by the powerful wish to broaden and to somewhat democratize the discourse.

At first the attempt to implement open public discourse about the quality of our built surroundings seems noble, but it is also very naïve and, in the worst case, counterproductive. It bears in itself the doom of liberal democracy—the danger of degrading to a mere form of nivellation of public discourse as the content of public debate is reduced and kept simple in order to achieve consensus. The Baukulturindustrie organizes an enormous apparatus containing campaigns, programs, seminars, or workshops, where young and old are taught what is good or bad in Baukultur. This even starts with pupils in schools, referring to the campaign *Baukultur macht Schule* (Building Culture Informs Schooling). It takes years to learn about the making of architecture,

[12]   Peter Conradi—who, by the way, is a social democrat—was the chairman of the Chamber of Architects and still is a major figure in German architectural politics. He was the key figure of the enquiry into the erman Parliament as to whether it was possible to establish a nationwide foundation for the promotion and implementation of Baukultur.

the sensibility for built environment, and the enormous responsibility that architects have. The Baukulturindustrie invites people to learn what is good and bad during various workshops, evening courses, and so on. The result is without doubt an extreme reduction not only of the complexity of building design, but also of its multiplicity. At the moment one can say that Baukultur is divulgating the idea that there is only one Baukultur. Might one go so far as to say that people are learning without understanding? All these attempts will not lead to democratization but to nivellation, because all the peaks are cropped and leveled to achieve a politically reasonable position accessible to basically everyone . . . Is it an exclusively German drama that *democratic consensus* always produces mediocrity?

There are some main strategies of the Baukulturindustrie to achieve hegemony. Let me describe a few of them:

Strategy of the Black Book
This strategy was initiated by Karl Ganser in the very beginning of the Federal Foundation for Baukultur. It is reminiscent of historic attempts from classical modernism like Bruno Taut's *Die Neue Wohnung* or Paul Schultze-Naumburg's infamous *Kunst und Rasse*—two books that, despite their different political directions, show what is right and what is wrong.

Strategy of Campaign-Form Politics
The central agencies pursue different aims and then start a machinery of public relations, flyers, publications, events, and so on, to reach the branched-out smaller units.

Strategy of Award Politics
This strategy is used in order to form or to teach "good architectural taste."

Strategy of Catchwords
These include *democracy, participation, sustainability, Verfahrenskultur* . . . They are repeated in a mantra-like way in almost every publication of the Baukulturindustrie.

Strategy of Networking
This strategy consists of the systematic detection and connection of all relevant institutions and authorities, but also the collaboration of the three sectors state, market, and civil society.

After having named and comprehended its strategies, it becomes clear that Baukultur represents the flip side of the neoliberal medal: a neoliberal project of hegemony in a certain field of discourse and practice. Concerning urbanism or city planning, the influences of neo-liberal hegemony are highly visible. For architecture within the meaning of spatial design, the matter becomes more erratic because it is problematic to amalgamate a political idea with an architectural form. But to search for neoliberal moments in statutory bodies, boards, or entities may be an alternative.

The vast lot of publications, reports, award characterizations, and newsletters around Baukultur are always the same—uttering no fundamental critique, providing no scientific approach. All the things issued by the Baukultur scene are on a very *industrialized* level (in the meaning of elaborated and *consumer-friendly*), so it is very legal to speak of the Baukulturindustrie. To give the *Baukultur* debate a scientific and critical background, this should be the aim. When we consider the origins of the word Baukultur, we will soon see that it comes from a background of both political *and* cultural debate, from debates starting in the late nineteen-seventies about a new relation between architecture and politics, as well as between architecture and culture, seeking to break up the limitations of the disciplines and reunite them under a new label, accessible to a wider range of *normal people*. In a yet-to-come analysis of architectural forums and the images produced, the intention of critically revealing the ideological function or quality of the Baukulturindustrie must prevail. An anti-ideological perspective toward architectural politics should be one element in a comprehensive analysis, to which this article seeks to make a humble contribution. After criticizing increasing centralism and monopolism, an attempt must be made to develop Baukultur as a fundamentally federal and decentralized model, or even as a kind of New Social Movement.

Gideon Boie

Born in 1975, Gideon Boie is a Brussels-based architecture theoretician and co-founder of the research and activism firm BAVO that focuses on the political dimension of art, architecture, and urban planning. BAVO's publications include *Urban Politics Now: Re-Imagining Democracy in the Neoliberal City* (Rotterdam: NAi, 2007) and *Too Active to Act: Cultural Activism after the End of History* (Amsterdam: Valiz, 2010). Boie teaches and conducts research in architecture criticism at the Catholic University of Leuven, Faculty of Architecture (LUCA).

Ole W. Fischer

Born in 1974, Ole W. Fischer is Assistant Professor for History and Theory at the College of Architecture and Planning, University of Utah. Previously, he has conducted research and taught at the Swiss Federal Institute of Technology Zurich, Harvard Graduate School of Design, MIT School of Architecture and Planning, and Rhode Island School of Design. Fischer is co-editor of *Precisions: Architecture between Sciences and the Arts* (Berlin: jovis, 2008) and *Sehnsucht: The Book of Architectural Longings* (Vienna: Springer, 2010), and he also authored the monograph *Nietzsches Schatten: Henry van de Velde—von Philosophie zu Form* (Berlin: Gebr. Mann, 2012).

Maria S. Giudici

Born in 1980 in Milan, Maria S. Giudici is an architect and educator. She has developed several large-scale urban projects in Eastern Europe and Asia with offices Dogma, Donis, and BAU Bucharest, as well as having taught core design studios at the Berlage Institute, Rotterdam, and the Barcelona Institute of Architecture. Currently teaching at the Architectural Association in London, she is completing her PhD dissertation at Delft University of Technology. Her research focuses on the construction of the modern subject through the project of public space.

Rixt Hoekstra

Born in 1969 in the Netherlands, Rixt Hoekstra is Assistant Professor at the Chair of Theory and History of Modern Architecture at Bauhaus University Weimar. She previously taught history and theory of architecture at various universities in the Netherlands and in Austria. Hoekstra studied architectural history at Rijksuniversiteit Groningen and at Columbia University, New York, and received her PhD in 2006 with the dissertation *Building versus Bildung: Manfredo Tafuri and the construction of a historical discipline*. She is currently working on her habilitation about the Italian philosopher and politician Massimo Cacciari.

Ana Jeinić

Born in 1981 in Banjaluka, SFR Yugoslavia, Ana Jeinić is a PhD candidate and Assistant Professor at the Institute of Architectural Theory, History of Art and Cultural Studies at Graz University of Technology. She studied architecture and philosophy in Graz and was a guest scholar at the University IUAV in Venice and Delft University of Technology. She is a regular contributor to *GAM—Graz Architecture Magazine*. Her current research focuses on the relationship between architectural concepts and political strategies in the era of neoliberalism.

Tahl Kaminer

Born in 1970, Tahl Kaminer is Lecturer in Architectural Design Theory at the University of Edinburgh after having served as Assistant Professor at the Delft School of Design, Delft University of Technology. He completed his PhD at Delft University of Technology in 2008 and received his MSc from the Bartlett School of Architecture, London, in 2003. He is a co-founder of the academic journal *Footprint* and author of *Architecture, Crisis and*

Resuscitation: The Reproduction of Post-Fordism in Late-Twentieth-Century Architecture (London: Routledge, 2011). He also co-edited *Urban Asymmetries: Studies and Projects on Neoliberal Urbanization* (Rotterdam: 010, 2011).

Ana Llorente

Born in Madrid, Ana Llorente is an art historian, art theoretician, and educator. She is completing her PhD dissertation at the Autonomous University of Madrid, after having been awarded the FPU Research Grant by the Spanish Ministry of Education. She has carried out her research at various institutions in London and Paris. Llorente has been a member of the Research Group El Sistema del arte en España, editor of *Revista Historia Autónoma*, and contributor to journals like *Goya* and *AACA*. Her research is focused on the history and theory of dress and fashion, architecture and visual culture, fashion photography, and fashion film.

Olaf Pfeifer

Olaf Pfeifer is a Berlin-based architect who was Assistant Professor at the Chair for Theory and History of Modern Architecture at Bauhaus University Weimar from 2005 to 2012. He had previously worked for Sauerbruch Hutton Architects, Meyer, Ernst and Partners, and raumzeit architects. Pfeifer graduated from Pratt Institute, New York, in 2000, and from TU Berlin in 1999. He was a member of the executive committee of the International Bauhaus-Colloquium 2009, *Architecture in the Age of Empire: Die Architektur der neuen Weltordnung*. His research is focused on constructions of authenticity, places, and atmospheres in and by means of architecture.

Andreas Rumpfhuber

Andreas Rumpfhuber is an unaffiliated resarcher and principal of Expanded Design, an office for design/research in Vienna. He is currently directing an Austrian Science Fund research project about the invention of office-landscaping and was Principal Investigator of the Vienna sub-project of the ESF/HERA-funded research on *Scarcity and Creativity in the Built Environment* between 2010 and 2013. He holds a PhD from the Royal Danish Academy of Fine Arts and was member of the PhD group at the Center for Research Architecture at Goldsmiths College, London. Rumpfhuber is the author of the book *Architektur immaterieller Arbeit* (Vienna: Turia & Kant, 2013).

Anselm Wagner

Born in 1965 in Salzburg, Anselm Wagner is Full Professor and Chair of the Institute of Architectural Theory, Art History and Cultural Studies at Graz University of Technology. He studied art history and philosophy in Salzburg and Munich (PhD in 2002), worked as curator, gallery manager, art critic, and editor of the art magazines *frame* and *spike*, and was Visiting Professor at Vienna University of Technology and at the University of Minnesota. He is the editor of *GAM* and of various other publications, including *Abfallmoderne* (Vienna and Berlin: LIT 2nd ed., 2012), and co-editor of *Was bleibt von der "Grazer Schule"?* (Berlin: jovis, 2012), *Staub* (Vienna and Berlin: LIT, 2013), and *Konrad Frey: Haus Zankel* (Berlin: jovis, 2013).

Oliver Ziegenhardt

Born in 1976 in Erfurt, GDR, Oliver Ziegenhardt is Assistant Professor at Bergische University Wuppertal, Chair for Architectural History and Theory. He studied architecture at Bauhaus University Weimar and Vienna University of Technology. His work focuses on architecture and politics, architectural politics, critical theory of architecture, pop culture, architecture, and "good taste." Currently he is working on his dissertation *Baukulturindustrie: Architectural Politics and Civil Society in Times of Neoliberal Hegemony* at BTU Cottbus.

IMPRINT

This book is published as volume 3 of the series
architektur + analyse,
edited by Anselm Wagner,
akk Institute of Architectural Theory, Art History and Cultural Studies,
Graz University of Technology

The editors would like to thank the rectorate of TU Graz for its generous support of
this publication.

Editors: Ana Jeinić, Anselm Wagner
Copy editor: Dawn Michelle d'Atri
Proofreading: Inez H. Templeton
Graphic design: Susanne Rösler
Design and setting: Toni Levak, with assistance of Ramona Winkler
Picture editing: Ramona Winkler, Michaela Böllstorf
Printing and binding: GRASPO CZ, a. s., Zlín

Cover illustration: Ludger Paffrath, Installation by Jürgen Meyer H.
for Calvin Klein, 2009

Bibliographic information published by the Deutsche Nationalbibliothek
The Deutsche Nationalbibliothek lists this publication in the Deutsche
Nationalbibliografie; detailed bibliographic data are available on the Internet at http://
dnb.d-nb.de

jovis Verlag GmbH
Kurfürstenstraße 15/16
10785 Berlin

www.jovis.de

ISBN 978-3-86859-217-7